WHERE,
WHEN,
AND WHY

BOOKS BY MARTIN MAYER

Nonfiction

        WHERE, WHEN, AND WHY: Social Studies in
                      American Schools
        THE SCHOOLS
        MADISON AVENUE, U.S.A.
        WALL STREET: MEN AND MONEY

Fiction

        A VOICE THAT FILLS THE HOUSE
        THE EXPERTS

WHERE, WHEN, AND WHY

SOCIAL STUDIES IN AMERICAN SCHOOLS

By Martin Mayer

Harper & Row, Publishers
New York, Evanston, and London

FIRST EDITION

D-N

LIBRARY OF CONGRESS CATALOG CARD NUMBER: 63-10753

IN MEMORIAM

Francis Lee Friedman

CONTENTS

INTRODUCTION

This inadequate book is the best try I could make in a year's time on an obviously impossible assignment. The report behind it was commissioned, and the book is now published, on the argument that you have to start somewhere.

Those who believe in the inevitability of events might be interested in the two proximate causes of the study on which this book is based: one, the reluctance of the Social Science Research Council to give its attention to secondary education; two, an airplane crash in Northern Rhodesia.

Because SSRC saw no "research problem," the American Council of Learned Societies, which usually fries other fish, undertook to sponsor an effort to reform high-school and elementary-school instruction in history and the social sciences. Applying to the Carnegie Corporation for money, ACLS was greeted with a question: "Admitting that we do have a crisis in social studies—what reason do you have to believe we can do anything about it?" At the suggestion of Carnegie's president John Gardner, who is herewith thanked (more or less), ACLS came to me and asked if I would be willing to take a year—or as much of a year as I could manage —and hunt for the people and the ideas that might work in the social studies the kind of transformation the mathematicians and scientists have wrought in instruction in their subjects in many schools.

Had ACLS come around a month earlier, I would have refused, because I had committed myself to a book on the United Nations. Two weeks of attendance at the seemingly perpetual wake at the Secretariat after Dag Hammarskjöld's death had, however, considerably diminished my enthusiasm for this project. Though I was still reluctant to attempt the ACLS job—partly because I knew the limits on how well I could do it, partly because it would inevitably make me an "expert," a condition I do not admire in others or wish for myself—the assignment did give me a self-respectable out from the UN commitment. And, of course, I was flattered to be asked.

The work for this report obviously built upon the three years I had spent visiting classrooms and interviewing educators for my book *The Schools*. On that project, however, I had sought a nearly random sample of districts to visit, making my selection basically for the reason that I had other work to do in a place—speech making, or information gathering on an article—for which someone would pay my travel expenses. Now I was looking for the best teaching I could find, and I solicited lists of teachers to visit from organizations, from people in the academic departments and teacher-training departments of universities, and from other teachers. I am particularly grateful in this connection to Charles Keller of the John Hay Fellows Program, whose fellowship winners—experienced teachers who have been given a year at a major university to refresh and solidify their academic specialties—testify to the taste and perception of the man who chose them, and to the high human and intellectual quality of American education at its best.

In the history of education, however, people working from within school systems have only rarely been the drivers or the leaders of forward motion. Rousseau, Froebel, Mann, Herbart, Grundtvig, James, Dewey, Thorndike, Montessori—all operated from outside the school machine. Even the exceptions—Pestalozzi, Edward Thring, Francis Parker, Helen Parkhurst—were pariahs in their own community and exerted their influence mostly through the support of articulate outsiders who had seen what they were doing. The recent math and science reforms were prepared, fabricated, and tested by the leadership, the ideas, and the work of university professors—though the intelligent assistance of selected teachers (selected by the professors themselves) was indispensable. Vigorous, imaginative, time-devouring efforts by scholars in history and the social sciences would surely be necessary if anything of substance was to be done in the social studies. So I visited universities, and talked with professors.

Between November, 1961, and June, 1962, I visited more places and people than I had thought I could in so brief a period of time —particularly in time encumbered by work on a number of inescapable magazine and other commitments. I have, of course, missed a great deal that ideally I should have seen, and neglected large numbers of people from whom I could have learned. So be it. As the author of *Fledermaus* puts it, *Glücklich ist, wer vergisst, was doch nicht zu ändern ist*—count that man happy who forgets what he cannot change.

Checking on the available personnel is, however, the easy part of the job of assessing the prospects for improvement in the teaching of social studies. More important is the question of the vitality of history and the social science disciplines themselves. The more romantic physicists like to say that what they have been teaching in the schools is "the revolution of 1928." Mathematics, too, has been over the last generation a rapidly advancing study. Programs to reform the teaching of foreign languages have been able to draw upon the study of linguistics, a plant in wild if not always fruitful growth. Only those who are secure in their accomplishments can make the generous gesture of seeking out what it is in their studies that can be taught to the very young. No opinion on what can and cannot be done in schools is worth much without an opinion on the status and vectors of the disciplines to be taught. Much of this book is therefore devoted to consideration of the disciplines, especially as they relate to possibilities for teaching. I neither assert nor deny any authority to express my opinion, and I invite those who are concerned about my criteria of judgment to induce them from the symbols printed on the succeeding pages.

The behavioral result of my year's work on this project was half a dozen long memoranda on people and things, which cannot be published (if only for reasons of libel), plus a report of about seventy thousand words to the American Council of Learned Societies and the Carnegie Corporation. What follows is similar to that report, though a fair number of changes have been made, and the specific recommendations for the expenditure of money have been eliminated.

The study on which this book is based was made possible by a grant from the Carnegie Corporation of New York. I am grateful to several people at both Carnegie and ACLS for their advice and for their consent to the publication of the material. Obviously, nothing in this book should be taken to represent the views of either organization, or of any person in either organization.

As the title indicates, this book deals with social studies rather than with socialization. School unquestionably plays a major role in what the well-intentioned dumbbells of the last generation called "life adjustment." It is in school that the American child tests himself with and against his peers, finds friends, moves from the protection of the family toward recognized status as an individual. This escape from the mysteries of adult perception to the inevitably like-minded world of his contemporaries is what makes school so enormously attractive to the child between the ages of five and eight; then the desire to establish an extramural role makes even the ideal school progressively less attractive to progressively larger fractions of the older age groups. The identification of "potential dropouts" in the primary grades is thus an unlikely venture, because children do not become potential dropouts until the school community seems less "real" to them than the world outside. (Intense financial hardship, of course, can make anything to do with food and clothing more real than anything to do with school from an early age; and repeated failure in school will diminish anyone's acceptance of its "reality.") Children who are active in the school's extracurricular program virtually never drop out. Socialization is among the first functions of the school, and activities that strengthen the school's corporate life—from student government to the safety patrol to the drama club to the football spirit to the junior prom—are usually worth the time they take.

Despite the fact that the word "social" appears in both, however, the social studies program has no more contact than the math program with the process of socialization. Adolescents do not "learn to handle their problems" in class discussion—especially not those "problems" which are important precisely because the child cannot bring himself to talk about them. Indeed, if these discussions were not carried on in ritually abstract, community-approved, meaningless language, they would constitute an outrageous invasion of privacy on the part of the schools. People can be committed to a mental institution only after judicial hearing, but people are committed to schools beyond the reach of *habeas corpus*.

Nobody who has passed in a state of consciousness through the rigors of adolescence can repress wholly the desire to help those who are following; and teachers, by becoming what the social psychologists call "significant adults" for the children in their classroom and by more deliberate exertion of personal influence, often perform an essential "guidance" function for schoolchildren. For some children, the teacher who touches the daemon will be the social studies teacher; for others, the English teacher; for still others, the science teacher; for a plurality, probably, the physical education teacher. The program is irrelevant to the purpose—though the teacher's method in presenting a program, and the atmosphere of the room, may be crucial.

Except where the socializing activities of the school can be used directly for instructional purposes—a condition almost certainly restricted to the relation between the political organization of the school community and the study of political science—I have omitted them from this report. Those who are interested in teaching children "values," which I am not (I feel like the Treasurer of Harvard, who wants to take an endowment "for the propagation of the faith among the Indians" and turn it over to the Indians "so they can propagate their own damned faith"), should concentrate their attention on this function of the school as a community. Children's values, as educator after shocked educator reports in a "research study," remain untouched by formal instruction; they are formed by the home and the street and the ethos of the community, inside and outside the school.

The mathematicians and scientists have thrown mental health out of their curricula, and the linguists are about to throw it out of the reading program. Let not the social scientists lack the courage to do likewise. Like the other disciplines, history and the social sciences are tools by which we organize the chaos of sense experience, and are thus emotionally satisfying to master. Like the other disciplines, too, they are either worth learning for the intellectual competence they bring—or they are not worth learning at all.

I

The State of the Art

"Events . . . will not be shaped by the deliberate acts of states-
men, but by the hidden currents, flowing continually beneath
the surface of political history, of which no one can predict the
outcome. In one way only can we influence these hidden currents,—by setting in motion those forces of instruction and imagination which change *opinion*. The assertion of truth, the
unveiling of illusion, the dissipation of hate, the enlargement
and instruction of men's hearts and minds, must be the means."
—J. M. KEYNES (1919)

* * * *

"Each of us has his own little private conviction of rightness,
and, almost by definition, the Utopian condition of which we
all dream is that in which all people finally see the error of
their ways and agree with us. And underlying practically all
our attempts to bring about agreement is the assumption that
agreement is brought about by changing people's minds—other
people's."
—S. I. HAYAKAWA (1950)

Linear motion is not normally characteristic of human affairs, and fields of academic study, like the fortunes of men and nations, tend to progress in complexly cyclical patterns of triumph and consolidation, decline and renewal. For history and the social sciences, the period of triumph came in the 1920s and 1930s, when great reaches of time and space, and tiny details of personal behavior, were opened up for exploration to prove the hypothesis posed by war and depression: that man's disasters were of man's own making. In those days it seemed obvious enough that "the proper study of mankind is man," and scholars thought Thurber was merely being funny when he wrote that only a man would say such a thing. Understanding could bring not only forgiveness, but remedy, too; social scientists would track down the elusive, necessary understandings, and schools would transmit them to members of the rising generation, who would grow into better human beings as the result of their education.

Whatever else they were, the 1920s and 1930s were periods of great optimism in education. Dewey, Russell, Montessori on her descent to mysticism, Lunacharsky, Jean Zay, the earnest reformers of Weimar—they all believed that schooling could reform society. In the universities, too, men were optimistic about what they would presently know for sure. The Great War had destroyed simple folly as well as simple hope, and the academics' faith in reason, the great legacy of the seventeenth and eighteenth centuries, was if anything strengthened by the disillusionment of lesser breeds. The attitude transcended political philosophy—the aristocratic pessimist Santayana, who could write of a hero nephew fallen with the Falange at the gates of Teruel, argued that those who did not know history were fated to repeat it, implying that those blessed with such knowledge could find reprieve from the judgment of time.

Then the decent belief that man was advancing toward understanding and control of himself was shattered by the liquidation of the kulaks and the rape of Shanghai, by Ethiopia, by Dachau, by Coventry and Hamburg, by Hiroshima, by communal murder in India and race riots in Belgium, by the great catalogue of horrors which is the history of the last quarter century. The social scientists retreated to the safe corners of their scholastic world—to statistical nit-picking, quantification, curve fitting, in fighting, all the modern equivalents of the once-scorned controversies of the patristic Church. "I believe," Augustine had written a milennium and a half before, "because it is absurd." A new generation of intellectuals wrestled with the evidence and logic—the "science"—of absurd belief. Among the more literary, a philosophy of "engagement" filled the emotional void.

The collapse of the pretensions of the social sciences caught American public education, which held a number of promissory notes from them, in a state of desperate intellectual poverty. Edu-

4

cational psychology and sociology had become disreputable studies, while the metastasis of the superintendency system had reduced official educational leadership to the level of municipal and state politics. Behind the schools, the American community saw itself no longer as a society with a world to win, but as a nation with a way of life to defend. In ludicrous but real terror at the dishonestly revealed but real treason of some clerks, the community lost completely its always insecure faith in the moral (as distinct from economic) values of education. American schools staggered into a period when, as Yeats had predicted, the best lacked all conviction and the worst were full of passionate intensity.

Nowhere was the disaster more damaging than in the "social studies" program. The false intellectual security of the prewar years had asked the schools to make children consider themselves and their society as the occupants of a small slice of space and time, the imperfect but potentially triumphant inheritors of vice as well as virtue. Phrases like "problem solving" and "critical thinking"— reasonable enough, if pompous, when the best minds of a generation believed that human problems were a set of situations in the game of rationality—now became shibboleths to guard the camp against the entry of bad news. Fortified against reality by their own incapacity, by the will of the community, and by the elaborate sentinel system of teacher training, the schools ritualized a program of "social studies" which, if it could not educate anyone, would at least prepare children to pass examinations and to show the surface attributes of "citizenship."

At the universities, the scholars were locked in the chambers of their own tragedies. They could not have cared less about what was happening in the schools.

CURRICULUM AND MATERIALS

American children who pass through the full cycle of elementary and secondary school (about 60 percent of all children finish

5

high school) will devote some of their time to "social studies" in ten or eleven of the twelve years. Despite the real independence of the fifty states in educational matters, and the formal independence of the nation's thirty thousand or so school districts, the social studies program is more or less the same throughout the country:

In the first three years, the child considers his home, his neighborhood, and his community.

Fourth grade usually concentrates on the home state, the rudiments of American political geography, and elements of American culture.

Fifth grade is American History, with some emphasis on exploration and settlement, and the colonial period.

Sixth grade is a hop-skip-and-jump affair through one or more regions of the globe, most usually Europe and Latin America.

Seventh grade is a maverick, and may include anything from "Guidance" to Geography, or the history of the home state (always the state; never the region, however arbitrary the boundaries).

Eighth grade is consecrated to American History, with some emphasis on the nineteeth century.

Ninth grade is usually Civics, though World Geography is not uncommon and there are places where Ancient History still hangs on.

Tenth grade is World History, usually optional; about half the high-school students take such a course.

Eleventh grade, for 90-plus percent of high-school students, is a third round of American History, now with some emphasis on the twentieth century.

Twelfth grade is typically elective, and about one student in five (which means something less than one in eight of all children that age) studies "Problems of Democracy." Among the other course offerings to be found here and there are Economics, Government, Psychology, Sociology, Foreign Relations, Modern European History, Modern World History, area studies, etc.

6

Textbooks used throughout the country are quite poor and quite similar to each other, with a few exceptions (among them, for example, Preston James's Geography, Ewing's and Stavrianos's World History, Graff & Krout's and Bragdon & McCutchen's American History). Text materials for the first eight grades are uniformly dull and without focus, often inaccurate, almost always misleading. Library resources vary enormously from community to community; they are often surprisingly good in slums schools (which inherited their books from the days when they served a middle-class clientele) and surprisingly poor in suburban districts (which have had to start from scratch in the last few years). The use made of library materials is a function of the teacher's ambition and quality, and will vary greatly from classroom to classroom within a given school. (The top is probably Phillips Exeter, where a library including piles of antique periodicals permits teachers to assign *real* "research papers" to adolescent students.) An increasing number of schools in prosperous districts are dipping into the flood of paperback books. "Heilbroner and Hofstadter," says the urbane Wayne Altree, head of the history departments in Newton, Massachusetts, "are gentlemen and scholars and friends of the high-school teacher." Among the many infuriating stupidities of the textbooks is their patronizing attitude toward the bibliography they recommend. Thus, for example, Allyn and Bacon's *Our World and Its Peoples* suggests John Hersey's *Hiroshima*: "An atomic explosion in the city of Hiroshima is an exciting but fearful story. Boys and girls can learn much from a reading of this book."

Maps for elementary schools are insufficient in quantity and typically trivial in content; many teachers rely on "news maps" of various sorts put out by nonscholarly services. In junior high school and high school the social studies room will usually have boxes of maps on window-shade rollers, hung above the blackboard, along a side wall, or (in luxurious installations) from the ceiling. They cover large areas in drastically small scale, and become useful only

7

when closely approached, which few students can (and fewer will) do during the course of a lesson. Each map is far more expensive than it need be, because schools (unlike universities) buy maps fully mounted and attached to rollers, rather than in sheets. Map transparencies, for use in slide projectors with zoomar lenses (enabling the teacher to change the scale of the map by a twist of the wrist), simply do not exist in American schools.

Films and film strips for use in the social studies program are cheaply and carelessly produced by the semiprofessionals of the "educational film" business, or slickly put together under the aegis of corporate public-relations departments. (An educational film may be defined, roughly, as half an hour in which bad actors mouth dialogue not in the least like real talk to reconstruct events that could not possibly have happened as portrayed. Nearly all such films are myth-ridden, presenting corporate enterprise as just like a kid's lemonade stand, or suggesting that legislation originates in action by the voters, who communicate with their representative.) Students of average intelligence hold them in contempt, and most teachers who use them do so from dogged devotion to a principle learned in training, or from the desire to get some time off from teaching. Here, as elsewhere, social studies is at the bottom of the barrel: there is a striking difference between the *Life* film strips for use in the natural sciences and the *Life* film strips for history and geography. The best educational films are the television network public-affairs shows; unfortunately, apart from the splendid *Twentieth Century* series, made available on a nonprofit basis by Prudential Insurance, few television films are shown in many schools. And only a handful of social studies teachers require students to watch public-affairs programs on television (though a fair number of English teachers ask students to watch certain plays). Time after time, the visitor to Problems of Democracy classes finds students and teacher embroiled in ignorant discussion of a problem recently outlined by *CBS Reports* intelligently and with a wealth of data.

8

For people seriously interested in the world around them, the most exciting sound that comes out of the little picture box is Aaron Copland's brassy orchestration of the great Quaker hymn (" 'Tis the gift to be simple, 'tis the gift to be free") that serves as a theme for *CBS Reports*. Distressingly few students—and frighteningly few social studies teachers—have ever heard it.

Magazines are commonly used—the news and picture magazines, *Harper's, Atlantic, Reporter, New Republic, Nation,* and *National Review* all make special efforts (and offer special discounts) to sell to schools. It is good politics for schools to encourage students to buy local newspapers (indeed, such purchases may be required by state law), and ambitious schools not too far from New York will arrange to purchase, at a discount, quantities of the *Times*. Generally, teachers are not conscious of the rootlessness and inaccuracy that characterizes the bulk of periodical journalism. One doubts, too, that much is gained by pointing out to students, over and over again, the simple-minded insight that different commentators and columnists seem to disagree on the truth and significance of statements and events.

On balance, the use of periodicals seems to strengthen the tendency to triviality and ignorance inherent in the "current events" approach to the study of society. In many schools, time is set aside for current events in social studies classrooms from fourth or fifth grade to the end; and teachers, struggling to hold the attention of a class, will cite the news in the effort to make the material of study "real, alive, and exciting" to bored children. There are, of course, admirable exceptions: "We can't be wasting our time with current events," says Marvin Lieske of Lake Oswego High School, just outside Portland, Oregon, "when we don't understand the background." The stress on current events is an interesting example of how superficial observation can distort thinking. Every good teacher relates the subject of instruction to something that interests his students, and occasionally points up its relevance to whatever it is that currently agitates the grown-up world. But currency to the good teacher is always the means, never the end—until the superintendent of schools gets means and ends confused.

TEACHING METHODS AND TEACHER TRAINING

Classroom work in the social studies consists of lectures, catechisms, student reports, and student discussions, in proportions that vary considerably from teacher to teacher, even within a single school. At a handful of schools (for example, Beverly Hills High School in the wealthy Los Angeles in-urb), teachers may arrange for their classes to have a period a week in the library; and in schools where experimental programs are afoot (such as Mt. Greylock Regional High School near Williamstown, Massachusetts, or Melbourne High School in Melbourne, Florida) groups of students will be freed from class attendance to study something. As an ordinary matter, however, students are not allowed to read in the social studies classroom, except for occasional textbook assignments. Some schools (among them, Chicago's good but much overtouted Dunbar Vocational High School) do not own enough textbooks to give one to every child, and the teacher perforce will make time for textbook reading in the class period.

Most teachers who lecture do it as least moderately well: an incompetent school lecturer, unlike an incompetent college lecturer, quickly learns about his inadequacies. In schools as in colleges, however, dramatic lecturers are not always good scholars, and the content of high-school lectures is often drastically inaccurate. ("The nobles of the robe," said a lively, energetic teacher in a West Coast high school, entertaining his class with the prelude to the French Revolution, "the nobles of the old purple robe, were the old aristocracy, who had control of the government. The nobles of the sword, who had fought their way up [slashing gestures here], wanted a share of the government. . . ." Then he wondered aloud

10

to the class why his visitor left after only twenty minutes of observation.) Some teachers who are basically lecturers will employ elements of catechism, pulling the necessary words or ideas or facts from students by means of questions containing broad hints at the answer; a fair number (some of these are definitely *not* good lecturers) will give a quarter to a half of the average class period to a lecture presentation of the material, with the rest for discussion or question-and-answer.

Extended question-and-answer periods are popular with the lower level of social studies teachers, because the questions to be asked are presented ready-made in the textbooks or the teacher manuals that accompany them. The main purpose of this procedure is to assure that students have read their lesson, though occasionally even a weak teacher will allow discussions to spring from one of the canned questions in the textbook publisher's package. Teachers with the necessary sensitivity and stamina can get excellent results with question-and-answer procedures designed to draw from a class some generalization that cuts across a number of lessons or even fields of study, or some principle implicit in the material. "If you transform fact into questions," says Peter Sugar of the University of Washington, "then you will get your student, and in a subtle way you will get your concepts." To succeed, however, this technique requires unusually intelligent teachers, students, or material.

Virtually everyone who has looked seriously into the teaching of social studies agrees that the ideal method of presentation is the group discussion. Its values are various. Students who prepare and present material themselves unquestionably learn it better than students who merely listen in. Because each student can operate from his own point of view, and must reveal it in the course of the discussion, the class and the work related to it are likely to be more interesting. Knowledge that he may be called on at any moment, and will be expected to make a contribution of some substance, keeps each student more or less alert to what is going

11

on in the room. And the teacher, hearing the part-conscious, part-unconscious results of instruction come pouring from her charges, learns something of what is wrong and what is right in the books the students have read and in her own presentation of the material. To watch a discussion class in the hands of a master teacher— a Henrietta Miller at Nicholas Senn High School in Chicago, or an Alice Atamian at William Diamond Junior High School in Lexington, Massachusetts—is to attend a drama of great emotional power.

The ability to handle discussion classes, however, is among the rarest of artistic talents, and the teacher training institutions have never learned how to nurture it (indeed, few professors of education have this talent themselves, or have analyzed its components). Most teachers fail from the start, by neglecting to require that students learn something before attempting to discuss it. Protecting their ignorance, and expressing the natural childish love of moral judgments, students will offer views on what ought to be or (in history) what should have happened, neglecting the hard questions of what is and what was. Typically, the reading that lies behind the statement is a textbook section, an encyclopedia entry, and perhaps a magazine article, all insignificant. The total misunderstanding of "democracy" which characterizes most teacher training leads in the classroom to the notion that on social questions one man's opinion is as good as another's, whether he knows anything or not. In Civics and Problems courses, and in current events discussions, teachers legitimately fear their own ignorance, and tolerate the most outrageous nonsense on grounds of "the child's self-expression." Uncontrolled, the discussion drifts off to religion, sex, parent-child relations, right-and-wrong, dressed in the shining paraphernalia of clichés which express sterility of mind.

One of the elements that distinguishes teaching from miscellaneous communication is the control of irrelevancies; the goal of teaching is to enable the student to control irrelevancies by him-

12

self. The art of group discussion is the control of the class from the back of the room, invisibly, with perhaps a word here and a word there. One of the advantages of the discussion method is that students occasionally make discoveries the teacher never expected them to make—but chance, in Pasteur's famous phrase, favors the prepared mind. Only if the class is kept looking for discoveries can the teacher hope to see results from the students' labors.

Teachers can control irrelevancy only if they know the subject to so great a depth that they understand precisely what is and what is not important in studying it—or if they have been precisely trained to use material of such force and simplicity that it drives the student's intelligence on a plainly marked through road to mastery. No teaching method can be said to work unless it presents the material in such a way that the student learns something of significance. But the range of subject in a social studies program is so great that no teacher can be asked to know it all to the necessary depth, and at this time the materials on which teacher training could be based simply do not exist.

No serious effort, then, is made to train social studies teachers. Of the men charged with carrying out this monstrous labor, the most able—an Alan Griffin at Ohio State, a Lawrence Metcalf at Illinois, a Donald Oliver at Harvard—live in a state of despair about the quality of the students, the quality of the material they will have to use in classrooms, the impossible magnitude of the job. The last half-century has seen a steady retreat by professors of education from the practical problems of teaching history and the social sciences, and now the retreat is a rout. Textbooks for teacher training must be read to be believed: all emphasis is on attitudes to be inculcated, "skills" (particularly "critical thinking") to be communicated, procedures for assuring healthy "group dynamics" and the like. Able men tinker with standardized tests and decks of co-variance cards appropriately punched, to determine

13

whether or not students are applying "logic" to problems in social studies. Meanwhile, teachers go out to classrooms with no knowledge whatever of how to present historical or social or geographic patterns in such a way that students will understand them.

As history is now taught, to give an example recently observed, students will not when they come to the sinking of the *Lusitania* make any connection whatever to the *Alabama* affair or the Embargo Acts—or even to the sinking of the *Maine*. The relation between "freedom of the seas" and American participation in international conflict is not something they easily discover for themselves, or retain well when it is simply told to them. (And the implications of maritime issues on a continental nation are thus a further step removed from teachable reality.) Somewhere there must be a technique of presentation by which a teacher can be assured that students will discover and keep such relations across time and space; but nobody in the teacher training field seems to be engaged in digging out and communicating such specific pieces of technique.

Since the turn of the century, there has been no systematic work directed toward improving simple efficiency in the teaching of history or the social sciences. In the absence of such work, the men responsible for training social studies teachers can scarcely be blamed for relying on incantation rather than on detailed analysis of the job, which they would have to perform for themselves. But there is something shocking about the idea that men who do not know how to build frame houses should put all their time into attempts to design skyscrapers.

From the classroom:

At Oakland High School in Oakland, California, a vigorous young man named Ronald Miller—who is an unpaid officer of the American Federation of Teachers as well as a social studies

14

teacher—is working with a refreshingly mixed group of middle-class high-school seniors (Caucasian, Oriental, and Negro, Jewish and Christian) on the history of China. He raps the class to order with the statement, "Let's go over the Ming Dynasty. . . . If there are no volunteers I'll call on somebody. . . . Yvette?"

"Peaceful and prosperous."

"That's real definitive."

A boy tries, "Well, it wasn't real prosperous."

"So?"

Another boy says, "More or less."

Miller nods. "Now we've covered everything. For the rest of the period, when we speak, let's say something."

Finally a girl offers, "Centralization."

Miller says, "All right. The Censor's Office. Now, who came to Macao?"

"The Portuguese."

"What did they think of the Chinese?"

"They thought they were barbarians."

"What did the Chinese think of them?"

"Barbarians."

"Good. So we have two civilizations, each thinking the other is barbaric. What was the relation to China of these outlying parts, the ones you read about in the news—Laos, Korea?"

"They were satellites."

"What was their responsibility to the Empire?"

A pause; Miller waits. A boy says, "Taxes."

"What kind of taxes?"

A longer pause; finally, a boy mutters, "Tribute."

"What class of people do you feel the West might have had some influence on?"

"Traders."

"Yes, but only in the port cities . . ."

"Now," Miller says, "what did the Emperor K'ang-hsi do?"

15

A girl says, "He issued the Manchu Edict of 1717."

"Fine. Now, what was that?"

A Chinese girl says, "It closed China to Westerners, and limited trade to Canton and Macao."

"The Canton trade was a very confusing thing," Miller says. "It caused great misunderstanding between China and the West. The Westerners expected to compete with each other. The Chinese thought the English and French and Germans should be able to control each other: since all Europeans look alike, the Chinese thought they should be able to cooperate. . . . It's a question of the lack of understanding of cultural traits. If you don't understand cultural traits, you can't be diplomatic. A Co-Hong might not work anywhere else but China—might not fit—might not be relative or germane to the society. . . .

"Now, would it be fair to say that the East India Company was the pusher of opium in China?"

A boy says, "It would be fair to say, but by definition it's wrong."

"What's wrong with it?"

Another boy explains: "The pusher is the little guy. The East India people were selling wholesale."

Miller nods and asks, interested, "What would you call the big guy?"

The boy shrugs his shoulders: "Mr. Big."

"Oh," Miller says, and gets back to work. "There was this scholar, a man of great integrity, a clerk—what was his name?"

"Lin Tse-hsu."

"What did he do?"

"He burned the opium. . . ."

"What was done by the treaty that ended the war?"

A boy looks up his notes and gives five basic clauses.

Another boy volunteers: "If a British subject killed a Chinese, he would be tried by a British judge. . . ."

16

Miller says, "Extraterritoriality."

Another boy volunteers, "The treaty established a new system whereby the losers had to pay for the war."

"Well," Miller says, "I wouldn't call it a new system. Goes back to Babylon . . . What was rammed down the throats of the Chinese was the cultural traits of the West. . . ."

At an upper-middle-class high school in a city between the Appalachians and the Plains, a tall, rather tired teacher is working with an experimental course for sophomores, introducing a brighter-than-average class to the mysteries of social science. They are in a section on Current History, and reading Vera Micheles Dean's *The Nature of the Non-Western World*, probably the most popular single text in high-school classes seriously considering Asian civilization. It is also used, of course, in wholly trivial classes. This one is now in a discussion, which a girl begins by asking, "What are the Formosans?"

"So far as we're concerned," the teacher says, "if you saw a Korean or a Formosan or a Chinese, any of these people we've been talking about, you wouldn't know the difference. The Formosans came over from China." This question answered to the satisfaction of the class, the teacher asks, "Why do we say, 'New Japan'?"

A boy says, "They've been trying to mind their own business. They used to be aggressive."

"Should Japan be included in the non-Western world?"

A girl says, "No."

A boy says, "No."

Another boy says, "No," and amplifies it. "They've taken up jazz."

Another boy tries, "They have a lot of bathrooms."

A girl says, "Well, they don't have a lot of things. My cousin's there. He says there's no central heating."

The teacher says, "Britain doesn't have central heating. Is *it* part

17

of the Western world?" Without waiting for an answer, he continues, "Even though Japan is situated in the non-Western part of the world, it is basically a Western country. Isn't this a sort of idea of the 'clash of cultures' we talked about before?"

". . . Right now, Japan is a quiet neighbor. Will it ever become an aggressor again?"

A girl says, "They trade with Communist China, and we don't do anything about it."

A boy says thoughtfully, "Before the war, I don't think anybody ever heard of Asia much."

The teacher says, "From what you know about the old China— somebody here mentioned *The Good Earth*—how would you contrast it with Formosa?"

A girl says, "The Chinese Nationalists have a very high life. . . ."

At Melbourne High School in Melbourne, Florida, one of the world's great teachers, MacClellan Fellows, a chubby, fast-talking retired dentist, is going over some aspects of Chinese life in an Asian History course. (Melbourne courses do not carry grade-level tags.) Fellows, who spent many years practicing in China, was teaching Spanish when B. Frank Brown became principal of Melbourne half a dozen years ago. He now teaches Chinese, Asian History, and math, the last because it interests him and he took two summers at the University of Illinois in Beberman's workshop, mastering a new approach to math. For his Asian History— China, India, Japan—he has written his own material, rich in observed detail of daily existence, poetry, custom, belief; humanity straining at the framework of scholarship, inartistic but immensely educational. He is a physically active sort of teacher, wandering around the room in incessant release of energy. His method, in history, is the rapid-fire lecture.

"Now, way back in B.C. they cut down their trees—poverty— they need anything that will burn. You've seen Chinese skillets—

18

well, they're so thin because of the fuel problem. That's why they sauté everything, because they have to cook it quickly. In the north they have the k'ang, a brick thing, with a top like cement. They cook on it, sleep on it. Once you heat these bricks they'll stay warm all night . . .

"Yangtze—literally, it means 'Dragon River.' It empties here near Shanghai, where I used to live. We used to have small gunboats in the river at the treaty ports, with the guns pointed at the cities to make sure the Chinese didn't kill the foreigners. I had a sailor in my office having some work done, he had to get it done in three days—bridgework—because he was going upriver. To Hankow, the Chicago of China. When I lived there, China had a new government all the time. . . .

"Just acres and acres and acres of white poppies, all in bloom . . . And cabbage, the poor man's food, full of vitamins. You make a jelly, it gets all nice and rotten and dry, smells to high heaven. It's like sauerkraut—it's delicious, we ate it all the time. . . . Mushrooms you buy in a drugstore. . . . We used to go out and gather bamboo shoots. The only poisonous snake in China is the bamboo snake. Like the copperhead here, you have to watch out for it.

"You know, with all those huge snakes, they have a different attitude toward snakes. Lots of families have a pet snake. I remember, the first time I ever had dinner at a Chinese house, I looked down at the table leg and there was this thing curled around it, grinning at me. I almost passed out. They said, 'What's the matter?'

"I said, gulp, 'Oh nothing, it's just—well, there's a snake here.'

" 'Oh,' they said, 'that's our pet snake. Do you like him?'

"I said, 'Ha-ha, he's nice.'

"They said, 'We're glad you like him. He's two hundred years old, he's been in our family a long time. . . .' "

PERSONNEL AND QUALITY

As measured by intelligence tests, the social studies staff is, next to the coaches, the weakest group of teachers in the secondary schools. In the colleges and universities, students concentrating in social sciences score less well as a group on intelligence tests than students majoring in physical sciences or humanities. (A very distinguished sociologist recently told the first meeting of a course in sociological statistics that "the work will be very simple: if you were capable of handling more than simple mathematics, you wouldn't be here.") And students taking an undergraduate major in education, most of them to secure licenses to teach on the elementary level, are as a group notoriously the bottom of the collegiate barrel in all measurements of intelligence. Group averages, however, are far less important than amateur statisticians believe. Though one could wish that standard deviations were greater in all three groups, the top of each group is large enough, and bright enough, to provide a high quality of leadership—if leadership could somehow be vested in the most able teachers rather than in politicians.

Roughly half the secondary-school social studies teachers majored in history or a social science at college. The rest divide up into graduates of colleges where students were allowed to major in "social studies," people who concentrated in other academic disciplines, and holders of degrees in physical education. In Louisville, more than half the social studies courses on the high-school level are taught by coaches; and it is true nationally that the coach is more likely to teach social studies than any other subject. It must be said, however, that many of the coaches are hard-working, competent teachers, whose necessary reliance on the textbook is less to be criticized than the lazy maneuvering on similar crutches to be found in classrooms taught by people who have all the "credit hours" that are supposed to assure mastery of the subject. Some of the best history teachers in the country started with an overriding interest in some other subject (most commonly, English literature); history enters into every serious study (especially, of course, the study of literature), and the teacher whose treatment of history is informed by the attitudes of another discipline may be far more interesting and effective than the teacher who loved the traditional plodding through names and dates and "trends" that still characterizes many college history programs.

American History is the field most likely to command teachers with intensive academic background in what they are teaching. World History is impossible as a subject for serious study—it is simply the title of a course (in colleges, now, as well as in secondary schools). The academic background for teaching it is, at best, European History, which means that Asia, Africa, and Latin America are taught, in the words of Larry Cuban of Cleveland's Glenville High School, "from the deck of a gunboat." (Though excessive reverence for the sensibilities of our underdeveloped friends ought not to eliminate the gunboat. Akbar was no more important to the development of India than Clive and Hastings and Cornwallis—the same Cornwallis, incidentally, who surrendered at Yorktown; Britain in the eighteenth century was not exclusively concerned with the American colonists.)

Teachers with substantial academic training in political science, economics, sociology, psychology, and anthropology can be found—in roughly that order of frequency—but it is unlikely that all the social science disciplines among them add up to as much as 10 percent of the total teaching staff in the secondary schools. Training in any one of these disciplines would be far more helpful than training in history for a Civics or Problems of Democracy course—except that the disciplined approach is officially discouraged by the educational leadership. These courses are probably beyond salvage, anyway. Edward Ladd of Emory University in Georgia

21

(who used to work in the Master of Arts in Teaching program at Yale) advocates separate licenses for teachers of history and teachers of social studies, hoping to produce teachers with sufficient strength in social sciences to hold the leash on the wild animals of the Problems course. It may be doubted, however, that an introductory year in each of five or six or seven social sciences will in fact add much to the competence of a teacher who must present unfocused material.

Yet the problems of limited background should not be over-stressed. No one is really equipped to teach *all* American history—close acquaintance with one or two large periods or patterns of change is really all that can be expected. The teacher who cares deeply about one aspect of American history—Jacksonian democracy, or the causes of the Civil War, or industrial growth, or international relations—will relate the whole story to that special interest, giving shape and substance to the course. Even if the educational leadership insists on retaining courses labeled Problems or Civics, a teacher can work from a single point of view drawn from one of the disciplines. The precise area of specialization—the discipline employed to focus the material—is totally without importance, but there must be a firmly established point of view behind the teaching or the entire enterprise is fake. As Purdue's Lawrence Senesh puts it, "even the most insignificant question must never be allowed to degenerate into 'current events.'"

Except in their attitude toward the World History course (which everyone hates, because nobody feels secure with more than a fraction of the subject), most social studies teachers are complacently dissatisfied with what they are teaching. "When you try to give them something new," says W. Burlie Brown of Tulane, discussing the teachers who come to his university for summer workshops, "they say, 'We can't do it and if we could *they* couldn't learn it.'" But where something better has actually been made available—most notably in the Advanced Placement program, in which high-school teachers are asked to work on a college level to win college credits for their students—a good fraction of them have jumped for the chance to teach it. Leften Stavrianos, professor at Northwestern and specialist in Balkan history and the Ottoman Empire, was given a Carnegie grant to develop a college World History course, and presently his mailbox bulged with letters from high-school teachers: "What can you do for us?" They are thirsty, the members of this fraction, for an intelligently chosen bibliography of books to read themselves, and of books to put in the hands of their students; at Advanced Placement meetings they pump their colleagues and the participating professors for titles, ideas, techniques. Margareta Faissler's *Key to the Past: Some History Books for Pre-College Readers,* in the series of little blue pamphlets published by the Service Center of the American Historical Association, has sold more than fifty thousand copies. There must now be a thousand American History classrooms where a visitor will find, in addition to the usual textbook, paperback books of documents, the Amherst series of pamphlets, Hofstadter's *American Political Tradition,* Leuchtenberg's *Perils of Prosperity,* Goldman's *Rendezvous with Destiny,* Bailey, Bemis, Palmer, and a handful of the other books particularly recommended by the leaders of the Advanced Placement program.

AP has been around long enough (since 1952 as a prestige-college experiment; since 1955 as an official branch of the College Entrance Examination Board) to demonstrate that teachers permitted to work on a college level with some of their students will draw better work from their other students, too. There is a ripple effect, downward to less able students working with the AP·teacher at other hours, outward to other teachers. In short, where leadership has been given by the colleges—and the AP courses, because they involve college credit, are written by a committee of three college and only two high-school teachers—the social studies teachers as individuals have been eager to cooperate, to supplement, to improve.

AP took half a dozen years to get started, cost the Fund for the

Advancement of Education a little money and the College Board a lot of money, and has by no means solved even its own special problems—a visitor to several dozen AP classes, in a sample weighted toward the better rather than the poorer work, saw as much weakness as strength, as much floundering as confidence, in the teaching. But, particularly in American History, Advanced Placement has shaken social studies staffs into an awareness of the high quality of work adolescents *and teachers* can do, if only someone will ask it of them.

II

The Established Subjects: Geography and History

Geography is the study of the spatial relations of phenomena at the surface of the earth, and as such it is obviously a very simple subject. Academicians with other specialties like to say patronizingly that "geographers don't really have a discipline," and in the years since the war such schools as Harvard, Princeton, and Stanford have given up their geography departments. When social scientists gather at meetings, therefore, it always comes as something of a surprise that geographers know so much that other people don't know. Whether or not geographers "have a discipline," they certainly have a lot of interesting ideas.

All social sciences are intellectually aggressive empires, and geography, despite its low rank in the university peerage, is no exception to the rule. Basically, the field breaks into two divisions:

physical geography (what is given on the earth) and cultural geography (what is done with it), which are obviously interrelated, though speculation on *how* they are interrelated is dangerous even for practitioners, let alone laymen. The more commonly known geographical specialties—political (what is the difference between Ecuador and Peru?), historical (where was Silesia when the lights went out?), economic (what are the natural resources of the Sudan?)—can be reduced to some mixture of physical and cultural and ought not to be regarded as independent fields. "Mathematical geography" is, like mathematical economics, merely an attempt to secure greater precision in formulation and flexibility in analysis through the use of symbols other than words. There is every reason why mathematics should be applicable to a study of spatial relations, and geography has been unnaturally short of model builders over the years. However valuable the mathematical approach may be in the future, however, it has not as yet developed to the point where one can seriously demand its introduction in the schools.

To say that geography has always been taught in American schools is to put a very low value on the word "taught." Marion Levy, a Princeton sociologist, says that one can always tell the difference between foreign and American graduate students in the social sciences, simply by asking some elementary questions in geography: the foreigners know the answers, and the Americans don't. Geography lends itself even more easily than most subjects to rote teaching and rote examinations, and American geographers, until recently, have been plagued by a simple-minded environmental determinism that fits nicely into the dullest sort of teaching procedure. Where anything more adventurous than rudimentary physical, political, and economic geography is attempted, it is customarily cursed (particularly in the textbooks) with the "other people are just like us" attitude that makes the real world simultaneously incomprehensible and uninteresting.

The general American failure to recognize drawing as an intel-

28

lectual tool means that children in the great majority of American schools never map anything themselves, though the home-drawn map is at least as important to geography as the laboratory experiment is to science. (There are a few schools where first-grade or even kindergarten children will make maps of the neighborhood, and very occasionally a teacher will work systematically on such a project, teaching scale, the use of significant features, and the points of the compass; in five years of visiting, however, this observer has seen the job done thoroughly exactly once, in a Detroit kindergarten.) Globes appear in the classroom in first or second grade, and are examined more or less casually. Teachers will post maps on the walls to answer individual questions, such as "Where is Cape Canaveral?" In second grade, the study of the weather in the "science" period will probably include some reference to what the weather is like elsewhere, and some explanation (often shockingly inaccurate) of why climate differs from place to place. Clyde Patton of the University of Oregon complains, quite legitimately, that the schools make almost no use of the weather maps available daily from the U.S. Weather Bureau, though both isobars and isotherms are notions easily within the intellectual grasp of second- or third-graders.

In fourth, fifth, and sixth grades children are stuffed full of geographic information, in a highly unsystematic manner. The continents and oceans are named, nations and seas are placed on the map; latitude and longitude are distinguished (quite ineffectively: confusion between the two is remarkably common, considering the clue given by the words themselves). Children learn about the Mississippi complex, the Columbia, the Hudson, the Rhine, the Danube, the Yangtze and Yellow, the Ganges, the Amazon, the Nile, the Congo, perhaps the Volga and (recently) the Mekong; the Rockies, the Appalachians, perhaps the Cascades, the Andes, the Alps, the Himalayas, and the Urals, which most students regard as great big mountains, because they divide Europe and Asia ("Russia spans two continents"). There are the Frigid, Temperate, and Tropic Zones; maritime and continental and "Mediterranean" climates; the Gulf Stream and the Japan Current. There are words: tundra, steppe, plain, swamp, pampas, desert, mesa, isthmus, delta, glaciation, peninsula. There are, unavoidably, the American states (sometimes with capital cities, even today), and occasionally the Canadian provinces (Newfoundland is now part of Canada). There are our Latin American neighbors (very few children have any notion of the fact that Paris is much closer than Rio to any place in the United States)—that in the North America-South America-Europe triangle, the side in "our hemisphere" is usually the longest. Serious examination of the problems involved in expressing a globe on a flat piece of paper is usually avoided, because the teachers do not know the mathematics of the situation, but both textbooks and teachers will mention that there is something wrong with the Mercator projection. Generally speaking, however, most American students grow up with a greatly exaggerated notion of the size of Canada, Greenland, Scandinavia, and Siberia.

Physical geography is customarily regarded as nasty and dull, and the landscape is peopled as quickly as possible, first with children, then with grownups and economic activity, which is explained by the presence of natural resources. Tokyo is the largest city in the world; the Dutch reclaim land from the sea and grow tulips; Egyptians farm the sediment deposited by the Nile; birds drop guano along the Chilean shore (this phenomenon is now mostly a matter between the birds and the rocks, synthetic nitrates having driven bird droppings off the market, but not yet out of the schools); America has everything, almost. Usually, the presentation is not much more systematic than that, and the elementary textbooks are too sloppily organized to convey anything substantial in the line of general principles.

Junior-high-school texts, though lavishly illustrated in four colors and provided with extensive glossaries and indices, are scarcely better than the elementary-school material, with the exception of Preston James's *Wide World,* which is far more sophisticated in relating lands and peoples. The James text has been difficult to sell; it was rejected in the Syracuse schools, despite James's connections there (he teaches at the University of Syracuse) because the adoption committee felt it would be too difficult for most teachers to manage. Other texts are organized almost entirely by nations, which is known to be a painfully inadequate approach to an understanding of geography.

Some geographical background is necessary for high-school World History and American History courses. By and large, teachers of these courses say that their students have never had any geography (which is not true). The "area-studies" approach to the teaching of World History, represented in the Ewing and Stavrianos texts, probably teaches geography, though both books are still too new (and too little used) to provide much evidence for the argument. American History texts are so crippled by the felt need to meet curriculum guides in school systems all over the country that they convey relatively little geography beyond repetitions of the material studied (but not learned) in elementary school. Such simple geographical notions as the line of the 100th meridian are rarely given any attention, except in schools in the area west of the line and east of the Rockies.

From the classroom:

In David Douglas High School just outside Portland, a gangling young man named Dale Jolly is working with a "slow" (under 100 IQ) class of ninth graders in a required Geography course. The class is pretty much a lecture, broken by opportunities for students to provide a missing word and demonstrate that they are listening, but nearly all the children are, in fact, listening to Jolly. He is an earnest teacher ("I am very interested in geography—very deeply

31

interested"), and obviously benefits by the general feeling in the ninth grade that "you learn something in Mr. Jolly's class." This class is learning something about race problems in South Africa.

"The tribes the Europeans first came into contact with were the Bushmen, and we'll go into their characteristics more when we study tropical Africa. . . . The Hottentots raised cattle and were less dependent on hunting. When the Dutch met the Hottentots they learned something unique—that property among the Hottentots was inherited through the women. The Dutch readily intermarried with the Hottentots, which is the origin of the Cape Colored. Many of these colored intermarried with the Bantu, a people identified by their language. So you find colored people with Dutch names and with beards, and, as we know from what we studied earlier, Negroes are usually not hairy. . . .

"Until Europeans were well established, they made no contact with Bantu. Bantus came under control of the South African government as American Indians came under control of the U.S. government. They were herded into reservations called High Commission territories. Today—now, understand this—three-quarters of the population is Negro, Bantu, and twenty-one per cent is white. South Africa is a modern industrial society, European. In order for South Africa to expand their economy—this is the paradox, this is the irony—they must bring the black man into the labor force. The general consensus is that South Africa does not have the resources to support a Bantustan, a separate African state within South Africa. But the two societies are very distinct from one another—in fact, in some cities a black man cannot go on the streets after dark. The government has a policy of retribalization, and the Bantu can work in cities only eighteen months before he has to go back to one of the two hundred and sixty-four reservations. . . ."

It is all quite simple, insistently stated; nothing more than exposure, of course, but a far higher degree of exposure than the brightest American ninth graders usually receive. The class finds it reasonable enough: this is secondary education. From his better classes, Jolly demands more. One such, later the same day, held a panel discussion on the relationship of water supplies in the Jordan Valley to tension between Israel and her neighbors, and meanwhile Jolly went over with his visitor the multilithed material he has prepared for his more able students to read in class (he does not believe in homework). Unit One deals with the earth as a globe, tells the story of Eratosthenes and carefully defines "oblate spheroid"; moves on to the geometry of maps, zenithal and conical projections, the different distortions represented by flat presentations of a spherical surface, and illustrates the transverse Mercator projection by the use of Army maps Jolly has collected. The next week the class goes into climate, learns the Köppen classifications and draws them on a map, studies Coriolis forces and deflections from the Equator, etc.

Place geography follows, beginning with the countries in the humid mesothermal climate of Western Europe. ("I always introduce place geography of a region before they read about it— there's no point in it unless you associate land-form characteristics.") Then Europe is treated racially and linguistically—the thirteen regions of the British Isles, the seven regions of Germany—and as the class becomes accustomed to Jolly's rapid but even passage over the surface of the earth there will be emphasis on subregional divisions—maps of the Great Lakes area, for example, to illustrate a trio of equations:

Mineral wealth + transport = manufacturing
Glacial soils + cool summers = hay and pasture
Hay + pasture + manufacturing = dairying . . .

Jolly recently gave one of his classes the mid-term examination from the University of Oregon's Geography 105, which is not a freshman course. "Lots of them," he says, "did quite well."

How much of Jolly's geography his class keeps is, of course, a

33

mystery. The great bulk of so detailed a course will inevitably escape. "I know it's advanced," he says, "but they can learn it and it's interesting to them. And it serves the real purpose, which is to get them interested in their environment."

ENVIRONMENTS

Of all the relationships that one might wish a student to be able to generalize, the easiest—the relationships requiring the least imagination—are those of contiguity. Unlike the other social sciences, geography deals constantly with precisely measurable phenomena. A sound sense of geographical measurement (which involves inevitably the important ideas of scale and projection) might make all learning in the social sciences much easier for all students.

Geography is in part the study of what man has done to his environment. The skyscrapers as much as the Palisades are part of the geography at the mouth of the Hudson River, and the sailor along the shore works from maps which feature water towers as much as land forms. Much of the history of man is the story of the changing environment: the grasslands become farms, canals link the rivers and oceans; forests vanish to meet the need for soil, then for housing, fuel, and newsprint; waves break on the breakwater rather than on the sand. What was once stuff in the ground, unrecognized and unimportant, becomes a "natural resource"; the rapids in the rivers, once a block to navigation, become sources of electric power. The ecology of the landscape changes drastically: the buffalo, the passenger pigeon, and the quagga disappear, man kills the insects on which the birds feed, plows the dry land to make desert, and irrigates the desert to grow tomatoes. The history of the barbed-wire fence is a vital part of the study of geography. No one can hope to understand what man does on earth without sensing man's impact on his geography.

Even more obviously, environment influences culture: Eskimos wear seal coats and Africans wear loincloths; people who live on seacoasts fish and people who live in river basins farm. Mad dogs and Englishmen go out in the noonday sun: man adapts to what nature provides. This sort of geography, with much emphasis on quaint customs and neat patterns, takes most of the school time now devoted to the subject; but there is really not much to recommend it other than its simplicity. Man's triumph has been, not his ability to adjust to environment, but his ability to change environment. As Preston James pointed out in his paper for the ACLS-NCSS book *The Social Studies and the Social Sciences,* southeastern China and southeastern United States are very similar habitats, but developed very different patterns of life. A belief in environmental determinism is usually an escape from an ignorance of history. The specific climate zones, land forms and resources of the United States are probably less important to its development than the fact that the place was virtually uninhabited—was a great stage for the play of nature, as Parkman so movingly pointed out—before the Americans spread across it. The key fact about China is the unexplained gigantic increase in Chinese fecundity in the eighteenth and nineteenth centuries. A geography that ignores history, as the essentially static environmentalist must, will be necessarily misleading. Progress in geographic education will require a ruthless destruction of the naïve environmentalism of the great majority of American teachers.

Finally, geography is a set of more or less arbitrary names—nations, cities, mountain ranges, rivers, oceans, etc.—set on specific places on the globe. The ability to place these names on the globe is indispensable, because they provide the reference points for the information from which, hopefully, geographical generalizations can be drawn. History, too, requires a sound knowledge of the location of events: students who know that two important battles were fought near Tannenberg (and many students probably *should* know that two important battles were fought near Tannenberg, why they were fought, and what the results were) can scarcely

35

make much sense of the facts unless they have a very accurate idea of where Tannenberg is. Place names cannot be learned except by rote, because they are arbitrary—but the omnipresent visual aid of the map makes the need for memorization far less onerous than it is in other fields of study, and the schools have many years in which to produce in their students a suitable aggregation of such "knowledge."

Geography is difficult to teach, because it is not a self-consistent discipline. It draws from so many other fields of study—geology, meteorology, anthropology, history—that its categories tend to be unstable. The contradictions in methodology and epistemology that beset the social sciences as a group are all present in the study of geography (as they are, also, in history). What appears to be a good teaching idea to the non-geographer often turns out to be misleading.

The psychologist Jerome Bruner, for example, was much taken with the idea of asking children to place Chicago on a blank map and explain why Chicago had to be just there. But this technique will not work at all for cities like Atlanta (chosen by a railroad surveyor, almost by accident, for a junction point), or for Los Angeles; Newark rather than New York and Oakland rather than San Francisco should have been the metropolis, geographically; Houston was made by the Galveston flood; Salt Lake City is the creature of historic religious hysteria and religious bigotry. Venice is incomprehensible unless you know about the mess that attended the decline of Rome; Paris, Berlin, Moscow are all rather unlikely, geographically, and Brasilia is impossible.

Similarly, Richard McCann of Meadowbrook Junior High in Newton worked out a splendid plan to have students determine regions for themselves, by mapping physical characteristics, population, economic use, climate, and transportation on separate transparent overlays. One group in his class, blessed with a Hawaiian member, chose the big island of Hawaii as its project and produced a perfect set of three regions. Another group chose the state of Massachusetts and wound up in perfect confusion.

Explaining Chicago and determining regions are both admirable approaches to the teaching of geography—but only if the teacher knows enough geography, or is following a suggested outline closely enough, to make sure that both the values and limits of the approach are sensibly conveyed to the class. Assembled and asked to think specifically about teaching problems, geographers can come up with even more interesting notions, as William Warntz, William Bunge, and William Pattison did in June, 1962, at the Endicott House meeting on teaching the social sciences and humanities. They proposed, as an activity for the primary grades, the use of solar readings to enable children to draw the line of the meridian of longitude on the school playground. Nothing could go wrong with this activity; at its best, it would make the classroom globe comprehensible, and at its worst it would pretty definitely guarantee an end to confusions between latitude and longitude. Clyde Patton of Oregon feels a good deal could be learned about climate through the study of heat balances in glass jars. A few dozen ideas of this quality, proved out in classrooms, with "hardware" or written material by which teachers could get the point across, might give an irresistible momentum to the drive to improve instruction in geography.

Right now, there is no momentum: each push takes a separate effort. The National Council for Geographic Education has for some years been publishing timid little suggestions—couched often enough in the aimless jargon of the teacher-training institutions—and the Council is now joined with the Association of American Geographers in an attempt to develop a high-school course in the subject.

Not all geographers are happy about this effort; Rhoads Murphey of the University of Washington, for example, wishes his colleagues would concentrate on elementary education—"not on highfalutin

37

concepts or academicians' principles but on very basic matters; not on information but on content." Even those who accept the notion of an independent high-school course are not always pleased with the approach followed by the committee. The committee of geographers formed by NCGE and AAG was asked only "to give guidance to the conceptual framework of the field." Actual development of teaching ideas is in the hands of ten high-school teachers, each of whom is trying to construct his own ten-unit course about the conceptual framework supplied to him. Each teacher has access to a university geographer, who will as a spare-time activity, an *ex gratia* gesture to the cause of education, attempt to guide the course. The upshot, somehow, is to be a television course taught by Clyde Kohn of Iowa, whose work shows few signs of the indispensable sense of adventure. To ask teachers to "develop these ideas that will exist in students' minds" is to invite mediocrity or worse; degradation factors enter the process even before teaching begins. Still, there has been some wit in the project (Stephen Jones of Yale, in a paper for the teachers, defined geography as "what geographers do better than others"). And in at least one case the geographers have been luckier than they deserve: Bertha Thompson of Talawanda High School in Oxford, Ohio, whose consultant is always on call (her husband is a professor of geography at Miami University), has worked twenty hours a day developing thoughtful units on land-forms (aerial photography plus a field trip on glaciation), distribution, climate, etc., reproducing maps and readings, investigating films. And at least some of the geographers must have learned something from all the teachers' repeated cries for quality material to give their students.

WHY TEACH HISTORY?

An acquaintance with the past is the sign of a civilized man. The lack of an appreciation of art, a failure to understand science, clumsiness of self-expression—any or at a pinch all of these can be forgiven to a man who calls himself educated. But the man who has no interest in any aspect of history is uneducated and probably ineducable. The absence of curiosity about the origin of what lies around him is the mark of a beast; the belief that everything in the environment can be explained by reference to the recent past is the mark of the child. Every social science is an interpretation of history (sometimes recent history), and its theories must square somehow with historical record or nobody will believe them. (Social scientists sometimes become quite confused about the priorities here, and insist that historical events are real only if they conform to the "laws" of social science.) Of all school subjects, history is the most nearly indispensable to education.

In recent years, however, history as a school subject has come under increasingly strong attack, from professors of education who insist that teaching must produce measurable results in terms of changed behavior and from professors of various social sciences who want some of the time now given to history for school courses in their own disciplines. The usual defense of history teaching is that it "develops critical thinking" or makes good citizens. But "critical thinking" as it is defined in the teacher-training institutions is simply unanalyzed solipsism (how odd it is that the doctrine of "critical thinking" took root in a nation which began its independent existence with the words "We hold these truths to be self-evident . . ."). And "good citizenship," of course, is merely the acme of acculturation, the willingess to adjust overt behavior to the verbalized code of the community. The two attitudes, incidentally, are logically contradictory, awarding primacy now to the individual, now to the group. Educationally, neither is worth a hoot in hell. But between them they have driven from the minds of many teachers the obvious fact that nobody can be seriously interested in anything without being interested in its origins, which are to be found only in the study of history.

39

In a remarkable article in a recent issue of the *Harvard Education Review*, Arthur Bolster of the Harvard Graduate School of Education was driven to the statement that history is worth studying only if it predicts the future, which is manifestly impossible. (Social scientists aren't very good at predicting the future, either, at present.) Rocking back and forth in the ecstatic casuistry of the Why Teach, analyzing other people's prose for (Lord protect us!) signs of emotional expression, educators often forget completely that everything in the human consciousness is the product of a chain of past events. One cannot hope to come to grips with any part of human reality without an examination of the past.

If one must talk about "values," the value structure taught by history is probably unfortunate. People are most likely to be interested in that part of history which is important to their own immediate situation. Ethnocentricity is so sealed into history teaching that its presence is rarely remarked: for Englishmen and Americans, the Spanish power was broken by the destruction of the Armada, and only a handful of specialists know the name Rocroi. Austrians trace the decline of Ottoman power from the repulse at Vienna; Spaniards, from the Battle of Lepanto; Greeks, from the War of Liberation. The relative importance of historical events to an individual does in fact depend on whose ox was gored; it is similarity of situation, rather than a defect in teaching, which makes high-school students in Atlanta chew over the Civil War in a manner almost identical to the approach of lycée students in Paris to the War of 1870. Ultimately, moreover, history knows no value but survival. "History to the defeated," as W. H. Auden put it, "may say alas, but cannot help or pardon." The Philistines, the Manicheans and the Habsburgs have a bad press, even today. It is hard to believe that none of this inherent success worship comes through in the teaching of history.

POSTS AND HOLES

Back in the days when the camel got his hump, history teaching was just so. There were four or five recognized divisions—Ancient in the Mediterranean Basin; Medieval European; Modern European (variously dated, most usually, in the United States, from 1492); American; and English. In most classrooms, the meat of the subject was a long string of names, dates and places, and events were usually explained as the result of activity by certain individual Great Men, whose lives were therefore of prime importance. Yet there is something wrong with this description, for a fair number of people seem to have received historical education of some quality. Macaulay was read and reread; Gibbon was admired; Michelet and Taine were well known; Parkman and Prescott and Motley, then Turner, Beard, and Bemis were abroad in the land. Anyone who has read Parkman or Gibbon or Macaulay will find it hard to believe that students learn more history from, say, a textbook by Todd and Curti than they would from such authors. Students of economics, sociology, psychology, and anthropology read Marshall and Keynes, Marx and Weber, Freud and James, Frazer and Malinowski; only in history is it believed that journal articles which correct data supersede books which offer explanations and that everything a student reads should be thoroughly up to date.

Still, by all report, history was dry stuff in American schools, and most people retained from their education in history a few bits of myth and a dust heap of unrelated information. "The Kings of England" became the symbol for time-wasting activity in schoolrooms. Together with those who wished to reform the teaching of history marched those whose utilitarian bias allowed no respect for history unless it could help modern youngsters solve modern problems. History teaching as it had been known sank gradually out of sight. Ancient History survives on a few hillocks and may even be

41

recovering (hopefully, with a heavy archaeological component); Medieval is gone forever; Modern European has been resuscitated rather forcibly by the Advanced Placement program, but is today essentially a private-school course; English is no longer regarded as worthy of a separate course. American is in the saddle, as it should be. Every state requires students to take at least one full year of American History, and two states (New Jersey and Colorado) require two years on the senior-high-school level. Many students take no history other than American History, and meet their social studies requirements with Problems courses, Civics, or something else. Something like half the high-school students sit through a course called World History, which in a single year drops its light mantle of coverage over Ancient, Medieval, and Modern, on all continents.

Teachers of American History probably know their subject, as it is taught in colleges, better than teachers of anything else in the curriculum. They have the chronological flow down pat, and the raisins in the dough come to the surface automatically—the Articles of Confederation, Shay's Rebellion, the dispute over the currency, the Alien and Sedition Laws, the XYZ Affair, the Louisiana Purchase and Lewis and Clark, the Embargo Acts, the War Hawks, etc., through the long year. Certain parts of American History are easier to teach than others—Marbury v. Madison, Jackson and the Bank, the westward movement and Manifest Destiny, the cotton gin and slavery, the Missouri Compromise, the rise of the Republicans and the coming of war, Reconstruction and the Grant scandals, industrial expansion, immigration, the yellow press, TR and the trusts, Wilson's New Freedom, the War and the League, prosperity and isolationism, the Crash, Roosevelt and the New Deal (we used to stress TVA here, but we don't any more), the Neutrality Acts and the Second War, postwar efforts to construct an international order, frustrated by the Russians. It all seems reasonable enough, but the fact is that it doesn't work. At

42

best, the result is a vague flow essentially homogeneous with recognized raisins, the knowledge of a few dates and a few names. There is almost no feeling of the texture of life as Americans have lived it, or of the residue of history lying all around. "It spreads out history like Stripe toothpaste," says Russell Bastert of Williams.

For a decade now, it has been obvious that even a great teacher cannot "cover"' even so limited a subject as American History in a single year's work at high-school pace. World History is manifestly impossible. Reliance on textbook courses—and textbooks by their nature must "cover"'—leaves the student of the modern history course with as many unrelated bits as the students of several generations ago. "Later," said James Bunnell of Atlanta's posh Westminster School, "they'll sit in a college class and hear 'Charlemagne' —and they'll think 'Oh, yes, I heard of him.' But that's absolutely all—'I heard of him.' " Now the bits may have fancy labels and pass as ideas (or "concepts"), but they still lie useless and inert in the mind until they vanish.

Most historians think they know what can be done in broad outline to improve both understanding and retention. The proposal has gone out to the educational public under Charles Keller's rather unfortunate word "posthole"; as a slogan within the trade, it calls for "the courage to exclude" (which implies, as Henry Bragdon of Exeter points out, "the courage to include"). What goes wrong with the standard American History course, even in the hands of an able teacher, is the insistence on cramming in too many different events, people, and trends. Instead, the diggers argue, the course should concentrate on perhaps half a dozen key periods, episodes, or themes, each of which can acquire a covering of associations to make it real. Ideally, students should learn enough about one of these units to "write their own history," presenting informed opinions about why events occurred as they did.

One does find teachers who work this way already—sometimes in department-strength groups, as at Mt. Greylock Regional High

43

School in western Massachusetts or Lake Oswego High School just outside Portland, Oregon; sometimes as individuals, like Henrietta Miller and Sadie Engelstein at Nicholas Senn High School in Chicago, Robert Rowe in Portland, John Anthony Scott of Fieldston School. The amount of work involved, in digging up bibliography and documents and reproducing selected passages, is almost brutalizing for a teacher who must also handle five classes every day; nearly everything that makes life worth living, apart from teaching, must be sacrified to it. Recently, paperback collections of documents, most notably the Van Nostrand Anvil series, have extended the possibilities of what a thoughtful teacher can do alone without killing himself.

To date, there has been only one systematic attempt to give teachers collections of such material and ways of presenting it. This attempt, still proceeding though drastically underfinanced, is the new Amherst series of units under the general editorship of Van Halsey, Jr., Assistant Dean of Admissions at the college and an instructor in the American Civilization course. Edmund Traverso, head of the social studies department at the Amherst High School until 1962, helped prepare the material and tried out much of it before it was distributed; and mimeographed copies were sent around the country to several dozen schools which seemed capable of reporting back intelligently on the results. At this writing, five such units have been completed—on The Ratification of the Constitution and the Bill of Rights, the Expulsion of the Cherokees from Georgia, Immigration, The Twenties, and The Thirties. On the average, each unit requires students to read about fifty thousand words of original documents in two weeks, which means about two hours a week of highly concentrated reading at the average speed of college-preparatory students. Nevertheless, some teachers who have tried the Halsey units feel that three weeks or perhaps four are necessary to get through the material. The teacher manuals ("the author's mind at work") are highly specific, dividing the unit up day by day and suggesting to the teacher some books he ought to read himself if he wishes to make intelligent classroom presentations. "The basic thing," says Peter Schrag, one of Halsey's even younger colleagues, "is to get the kid asking the right kind of questions. The real hard thing is to keep them from asking too big questions."

The introduction to the student in the first of the units (on the Constitution) is ill-written but worth quoting:

. . . By and large the readings will not tell you what "happened" in the same way as a textbook would. Instead, you will be asked to do very much the same thing that the historian does. You will read documents and you will be asked to formulate your own history of the period.

In doing this work, it is generally assumed that high-school students are capable of mature work, that they need not be led by the hand. Consistent with this idea, this manual provides you with a short bibliography. Look it over before you proceed far into the unit. You are not responsible for reading these works but it is hoped that you will use the bibliography to amplify points which you feel are not sufficiently clarified in the assigned readings. In addition, you will find a brief chronology of events at the back of the manual. You need not memorize it but you must have it in mind as you do your work.

These Halsey units will be published, like the earlier series of Amherst problem pamphlets, by D. C. Heath and Company. Halsey and his colleagues have some feeling that the publication is a touch premature—that another year's experience in teaching the material might have made major improvements possible—but the working group needs the money from publication if it is to continue, and the first printings will not be so large as to prohibit changes as experience accrues. These units, incidentally, should not be confused with the earlier Amherst series of problems-in-history pamphlets, which were written for colleges but have been the mainstay of the Advanced Placement Program. The new series is considerably more scholarly, deals with topics rather than with problems, and considers at every turn the need to guide teachers who are not so well acquainted with the material as the college instructors who use the earlier Amherst pamphlets.

From the classroom:

At Nicholas Senn High School, in the middle-class northern tier of Chicago, Mrs. Henrietta Miller, a large, cheerful, tolerant lady who has probably done more with the Advanced Placement program than any other public-school teacher in the country, is working with her twenty-five senior-level, AP Modern European History students. In the next room, Sadie Engelstein, thinner, younger, equally cheerful and intelligent, is giving the junior-level American History AP students a sense of what it means to work from documents and first-class historical writing rather than from textbooks and encyclopedias. Mrs. Miller inherits the benefits of Miss Engelstein's work, and appreciates them; their students enormously appreciate both teachers. Neither is much impressed with IQ measurements or other standard criteria for entrance to AP work; every year, they try a few children whose measured IQ is under 100 but who seem to have the necessary interest to keep up with college-level work. The method employed starts with catechism in Miss Engelstein's class and works ahead to free discussion toward the end of the American History year and throughout the Modern European course.

Like good conversation, Mrs. Miller's class is hard to report: it is a chiaroscuro of argument, fact, objection, citation. Class sessions are by no means an everyday matter; students in Mrs. Miller's AP course spend most of their class time reading, preparing for the next discussion. This one deals with the political and economic situation in England, France, and Germany about the turn of the century:

"Well, for one thing, the socialism that grew up in Germany was of a more passive sort. . . ."

46

"I don't see how you can compare. England was unique. France had been unified many years before, Germany only in 1871."

"France was a Republic because the monarchists weren't united, they fought with each other."

Mrs. Miller interrupts: "Do you think if the monarchists had been able to get together France wouldn't have been a Republic?

The students continue:

"Yes, I do . . ."

"Whether they were united or not, people were under the same conflicts. . . ."

"We've got the Reform Bills in England. 1832, 1871. Why didn't the Industrial Revolution do the same thing in Germany?"

"When *were* the trade unions legalized in the different countries?"

". . . In 1900, the SPD was the most powerful party in the Reichstag, and the Labour party wasn't anything. Why was Britain so far advanced?"

"Well, the Reform Bill of 1832 wasn't passed until England was on the brink of revolution. . . ."

"What were the people in a position to demand in Germany?"

"The heritage is so different. England was different from France and Germany. . . ."

"The Germans had lived in princely states, they were used to absolute rule. . . ."

At the break, half a dozen members of the class gather around Mrs. Miller's desk, to borrow her books. Several individual arguments persist as the class drifts slowly out into the halls.

In an upper-middle-class suburb of Seattle, a bright class of twenty-six seniors is struggling to answer a young teacher's question on the economic impact of the Treaty of Versailles:

"From my reading," a boy says, "I don't think the League of Nations was the sort of organization they wanted. It didn't accomplish what they wanted it to accomplish."

47

"But, George," says the teacher, "what was the *economic* impact?"

"Well, they made so many little countries."

Another boy tries, "Well, they just stripped Germany down, they stripped Austria down, they couldn't live, and in my opinion that was the cause of World War II."

A girl says, "When people are suppressed they'll go for anything —like in the French Revolution, a man comes along with an idea they thought would help them. . . ."

Another girl: "People who think they've been treated badly will react more strongly."

"The French," says yet another girl, "got their coal fields back, their minerals. They could ship out of the country to people who needed minerals."

"Britain was upset," says another girl, "because they weren't top nation in the war."

The teacher, a handsome young man, bitter and intelligent in the teachers' lounge and rather serious about teaching, remains surprisingly calm in the face of this ignorance. There is, alas, a point he wants to get through: "Remember the democratic spirit that was growing in Europe all through the nineteenth century. Do you think that had anything to do with Wilson's Fourteen Points?"

"Yes."

"Was the Versailles Treaty written in this spirit?"

"No."

"What's going to be the result among the people of Europe who wanted the Fourteen Points?"

A boy says, "They're going to be disappointed."

The teacher nods happily. "Disillusioned . . ."

From the blackboard, chalk names stare out at the students:

> Freud
> Pavlov
> Darwin

Einstein
W. James
Hegel
Nietzsche

The teacher says cheerfully, "You won't have time to read them or the things based on them, but you ought to know something of what they had to say. . . ."

PROSPECTS AND PERILS

Though almost no money has been spent on the problem (Boyd Shafer of the American Historical Association reports an annual budget of $10,000 to $15,000 for teacher retraining), history teaching has certainly been improving over the last four or five years. Paperback books have made intelligently written history available to whole classrooms of students; even the textbook publishers have put out a fair number of books of readings and documents. (Leften Stavrianos feels that if a school system cannot afford both his new World History textbook and the book of readings he put together to accompany it, they should buy the book of readings and forget the text.) Yet the improvements which have occurred so far merely reveal the enormous distance still to be covered.

Browsing through most of the books of readings and documents issued in the last few years is a discouraging experience. Selections are highly conventional; often enough, they merely illustrate where the textbook writers (or editors) got their dull ideas. Like the textbooks, the books of documents mostly "cover" large stretches of time, which means that the juice has to be squeezed out of each topic and period. Distinction between contemporary documents and historians' descriptions is often poorly made, and the student can go through many of these books very carefully without ever sensing that the world looked much more complicated to the participants

49

in historical events than it does to historians writing about them. The introduction of the term "social Darwinism" to the high schools, for example, probably convinces most students that Sumner and his contemporaries thought they were engaged in promoting Darwin, whom most of them detested as antireligious. (The editors of the 1962 *Yearbook of the National Council for the Social Studies*, interestingly, chose a quote from Sumner, the most doctrinaire of American theorists and political commentators, to illustrate distinguished advocacy of "critical thinking.") A bright student in a good teacher's class asked anxiously how the late nineteenth-century clergy could be pro-Darwin in social thought and anti-Darwin in biological thought—and the question was taken as proof of late nineteenth-century hypocrisy rather than as an example of confusion resulting from the projection of a historian's label back to the consciousness of people living in the period the label described. Nobody had the vaguest notion of the fact that "the survival of the fittest" was Spencer's version of Lamarck, and preceded Darwin by some years. Much more careful and imaginative selection of documents, based on actual teaching in the Pittsburgh schools, has been done by Edwin Fenton of Carnegie Tech, and will be published shortly by Scott, Foresman & Co.

There is also considerable danger that the new emphasis on documents and original sources will deteriorate to the pedantries of historiography. Undoubtedly, a scholar needs the picky little tools—the camel's-hair brushes of the archaeological dig—to find the original colorations of truth for the bits in his mosaic. Students, however, can operate with shovels, and in some instances steam shovels. For students, the purpose of reference to original documents is not to uncover the truth, but to convey the flavor of a time and to allow induction rather than memorization of historical generalizations. To work with documents, students need a good deal of information. One class in a good school, for example, had been given the Tanaka Memorial to read and then told, "You are the British

Cabinet in 1924, and a copy of this document has just come into your hands. What should you do about it?" A girl said plaintively, "Mr. ———, we don't *know* enough to know what we should do." (Neither did the British Cabinet of 1924, but that was not the purpose of the lesson.)

Working with original materials and demanding induction requires a fine eye for what is significant. History is something more than the current events of the past. Accuracy is always important, but only to the degree that inaccuracy distorts explanation. (There is even a case to be made for the proposition that the student who knows no more about Greece than Lorenzo knew comes out ahead of the game: the truth about fifth-century Athens may be less important than what Renaissance Italy or nineteenth-century England believed about fifth-century Athens.) The art of history teaching is not to get students to write "their own" history, but to get them to write intelligent history; and to this end the teacher can and should rig the situation.

Finally, the utilitarians can do great damage to the substance of history teaching by twisting to their own purposes the recognition that the whole field of knowledge cannot be "covered'" in high-school courses. Writing of "the Information Explosion," the Foreign Relations Project of the North Central Association points out that "even if the teacher had a maximum amount of time at his disposal, all of the material a student should know could not be covered." This statement, the pamphlet adds, "implies that very careful selection must be made of subject matter." But the conclusion is contradictory to the premise: "careful selection" means giving the student the material he should know. If he cannot have everything he should know, the bounds on selection should be lifted, for many hundreds of different selections can all be valid. That which relates most directly to current events may turn out to be the least valid: look how the Middle East dropped out of the news when we found we had too much rather than too little oil.

51

History instruction today needs to be opened at the seams. Much too much of it consists of the teaching of approved verbalisms, which are usually of service only for the purpose of answering examination questions, and tell almost nothing about the quality of life in the period. (How much we could gain, for example, by a three-page pamphlet on the role of the crossing sweeper in the nineteenth-century, to call vividly to mind the fact that there was horse manure on the streets.) It picks up its explanations at random, without defining "the forces" at work. And it is all far too much alike, cutting narrowly across differences in place, teacher interest, social level, ability level. Vocational schools should have a history of technology; Negroes, lacking the background of race pride that kept the immigrants afloat, could use school-taught Negro history; all teachers need the chance to teach what most interests them, out of any period, any place, in any focus. It does not matter in the slightest whether the student works on the history of France or the history of China, provided that he gets into his subject deeply enough to understand what was going on in, say, 1789 or 1911. Within the history of France, it is utterly unimportant whether two weeks are allocated to Richelieu and one day to Dreyfus, or one day to Richelieu and two weeks to Dreyfus—nothing is fatal but the attempt at equal, even coverage. With the enormous quantity of significant history to be studied, it is puerile to believe that teachers left to their own devices will teach trivial subjects. The danger is that they, and the material they use, will emphasize what is trivial in significant subjects, simply for lack of thought and help from the community of historians.

From the classroom:

Perhaps the most remarkable place in American public education is the Zilda P. Sibley Museum in the Walnut Hills School, otherwise an unremarkable modern single-story elementary-school building, in Baton Rouge, Louisiana. The room was Mrs. Sibley's sixth-grade classroom, and on her death in January, 1961, a grateful community set it aside as headquarters for the Junior Archeological Society which she and her husband, J. Ashley Sibley, Jr., had founded with the boys of the Baton Rouge school system in April, 1959. Membership in the society is open to all boys from sixth to twelfth grade in the Baton Rouge area, provided they have above-average marks in their schoolwork (membership in the society takes a good deal of time, which students with below-average marks probably should employ in other ways), and provided they pass a rather rigorous six-week training course. The society, says the preface to its magazine, *The Junior Archeologist*, "is a scientific organization established for the study of man through archeology, anthropology and related sciences." Its faculty advisers, one of whom usually attends the two-hour Thursday-night meetings, are Fred Kniffen and William Haag of Louisiana State University. In addition to the Thursday meetings at the museum, the society holds fairly frequent Saturday meetings and goes on monthly digging expeditions. Very few people know so much about Indians, or about archeology, as the two dozen young members of this society.

Archaeology was the Sibleys' hobby. They made digging trips to Mexico, and at home they would take their students out on weekends to nearby sites. (Sibley himself was then a junior-high teacher; he moved over to elementary school after his wife's death.) The product of these excavations inevitably found its way back to the classroom, and formal organization followed at the request of the students (who also contributed some of the boys'-club Indian aspects, with clans, secret rituals and handshakes, Chief, Shaman, Signal Sender, Wampum Keeper, Notch Maker, etc., as well as scholarly reports). What is in the Zilda P. Sibley Museum is the Sibleys' own collection of artifacts dug up and purchased in Mexico and in the lower Mississippi Basin, plus the results of the boys' own work. Everything is classified in a scholarly manner. Where examples of pottery or implements have not yet been found *in situ,* the boys, using tools the Indians used ("except we had a rolling pin for ceramics"), have made them according to pictures in archaeological reports.

A twelve-year-old takes the visitor around the room, pointing out first the Mexican material, then the collection of "projectile points" (serious archaeologists do not use the word "arrowheads"), gathered by the boys themselves. Every member must also make arrowheads, using Indian tools, to the satisfaction of his fellows. The various sites the club has dug are described—the Marksville site, Coles Creek, the Menefee site (named for the boy who found it on his father's farm, and thereby crashed into the society under age), Poverty Point. "Poverty Point," says a twelve-year-old, "was really one of the most mysterious cultures we know of in the state of Louisiana." The remains of each site have been classified according to recognized culture patterns, and the boys have made enlarged drawings of the stratigraphy at the dig, complete to details of the pottery. ("Charley Waghorn and Toby Steiner are working in this culture period.") At one of the sites, one pair of boys was lucky enough to find a full skeleton in a burial mound; it rests beside the front door to the museum, reassembled in a box of dirt with the artifacts around it, just as they were discovered. The first duty of the secretary of the society is, he says, "to read and keep up with all writing about archaeology, so I can advise members on the best proceedings." A library of about fifty books, and sets of half a dozen journals, takes up one corner of the room.

This Thursday-night meeting features an address by a young man introduced as "Richard Dick Warren," a handsome, crew-cut LSU sophomore majoring in anthropology and archaeology, who speaks about the Indian cultures and remains in his native Ozark Highlands area of Missouri. He stands behind a table on which he has lovingly spread out his own collection of projectile points, classified by site and period (Paleo, Archaic, Early Woodland, Middle Woodland [Hopewellian], Late Woodland, Mississippian, Historic). He commits what educational theorists insist is the most common and worst error of the inexperienced teacher—he goes into everything in great detail—and the boys love it. They are still full of beans at nine o'clock, when the honking of parental chauffeurs outside on the driveway begins to break up the meeting.

"Deer and turkey," Warren says, "were favorites of these Indians, if the bone count can be relied upon. . . . What paleo we have is all from the Highlands, but we don't know. They hunted the mastodon. . . . In a pocket of Renaud Cave, we found a pit with perfect stratigraphy, and we cut a very nice trench. Most sites are gutted in Missouri—everybody and his brother knows what an arrowhead is, whether he's got a site on his property or not. . . . This is Hopewellian pottery. The Hopewellian people disappeared, we don't know why. It's altogether possible that it wasn't the people that migrated but the ideas, which came down from the Ohio. I didn't really figure that out myself, I had to read up about it. . . ."

At the end of the talk, the boys cluster around the table to admire the arrowheads. A thirteen-year-old notes that the paleolithic arrowheads are much more finely made than the rest, and wonders why. "Did the making of the points have to do with the kind of animals they hunted?"

"I don't think so," Warren says. "It was the type of people, their way of living."

"Well, I think the paleo people perfected their points because they had a lot of time. After they killed a mastodon, they could sit around for a week eating him. When you hunt rabbits, you have to be ready to waste a lot of points. . . ."

Warren and Professor Haag (one of whose specialties, a boy remarks, is the identification of archaeologists previously at a site from the labels on the whiskey bottles) give the boy delighted smiles, and accept the hypothesis. . . .

55

ARCHAEOLOGY AS AN APPROACH

The establishment of a firm chronology with a fixed base point (in Christian countries, the birth of Christ) is one of the great triumphs of civilization. Young children cannot handle this idea at all. They take themselves as the base point, and adopt much the same attitude in looking backward and forward; and their time scale relates closely to their age. Study of a small and misleading sample (my son and his friends) produces the hypothesis that words like "before" and "after" are very confusing to the child looking back into history (which interests him a good deal). "Before" is something nearer to him; "after" is something further from him. Thus, knowing full well the actual relationship in time, he will say that "Columbus discovered America after the Civil War."

Until these confusions are straightened out—which for most children probably does not happen before the middle years of the elementary school—history cannot be sensibly taught. Even when the child does have a sense of time flow (which may arrive from insistence to the same myths about the same holidays at about the same stage in each school year), premature exposure to dates and wide-ranging historical sequences may leave him uninvolved, knowing his facts but bored before he begins. What passes for history in the fourth and fifth grades, whether it is stories about little boys and girls in Colonial America or the building of idealized little Agoras or medieval castles, leaves no residue of understanding. There is a suspicion here that the route to a meaningful study of history lies (logically and psychologically as well as chronologically) through the study of archaeology.

Precise time placements are usually impossible in archaeology (even Carbon-14 leaves you a lifetime off the mark, at best), so there are no dates for children to memorize for examinations. Time sequence, however, is given in a wholly visible form—through the successive strata on the site. (Admittedly, no site does present the kind of stratigraphy diagrammed in the final report on the dig; but children need not know that at the beginning, any more than the early archaeologists did.) And the question of what one can or cannot say, on the basis of the mud walls, bone pits, ceramics, stone and/or metal objects in the ground, makes an excellent introduction to the infinitely tricky business of the nature of evidence—in the social sciences as well as in history. Preliterate, preferably vanished societies make fine pedagogic models precisely because they offer so little evidence. Everything is relevant, and at the same time the boundary between logical reconstruction and pure speculation is relatively firm. Moreover, the material is intrinsically interesting.

Far and away the most interesting moment at the Endicott House conference in June, 1962, was the presentation of the report from "Group A"—the historians Charles Keller and Leften Stavrianos, the art historian Joshua Taylor, the classicist Gerald Else, the novelist Mark Harris, the sociologist Robert Havighurst, the psychologist Richard Jones, the political scientist Norton Long, the geographer William Bunge, and Evans Clinchy of Educational Services, Inc. The group proposed a six-unit elementary-school sequence, including "Bones and Stones" (which would involve actual "excavation" of a previously prepared box with objects shaped to resemble those found at Choukoutien; films on primate life, on the actual dig at Choukoutien and on the Bushmen; an attempt to organize playground activities without the use of language, and the invention of a language); a unit on nonliterate agriculture communities (comparing what is known about prehistoric Jericho and the Hopi culture, again using "hard evidence" wherever possible); and a unit on the first cities (Ur of the Chaldees and Lagash are proposed, with emphasis on the beginning of written language, technology, cultural diffusion). Not

57

everything in such a sequence would work (the introductory first-grade unit on "space and time" has a suspiciously adult look to it, and might compound confusions); not everything in the proposal is historically or anthropologically valid; and many other patterns of elementary instruction can be imagined. But the scholars assembled at Endicott House felt their hearts lift as the sequence of these units was described, in a brisk, matter-of-fact manner by Evans Clinchy; surely, teachers and children should have a chance to share this excitement, if they can.

And, indeed, they may. It was this report which started Douglas Oliver of Harvard on his more refined and careful program of anthropology in the elementary schools, which will be met again in Chapter IV.

III

The Older Social Sciences:
Government
and Economics

Government, now so elegantly known as "political science," was one of the earliest academic studies of man. Among the first uses of written language, once the gods had been propitiated, was the preservation (and presently codification) of laws and customs. To be the lawgiver was the most godlike of kingly attributes; Solomon stands highest in public esteem on the roster of the Kings of Israel. In the time of the Greeks, the practice of politics came to be regarded as the highest duty of the leisured intellectual. Plato's *Republic* is the most advertised document surviving from Hellenic antiquity. Together with Pericles' lyrical funeral oration (which supplied the ends required by teleology) and Aristotle's *Politics*, it has exerted for two millennia a gravitational pull on political thought. The right quote from *The Republic* will be regarded as legitimate grounding for an argument, even today.

Law, personal service, and taxation are the great issues in the long dialectic of sovereignty and consent which is the history of political theory. But the relationship of this dialectic to the realities of social organization has never been very close, if only because the content of the key words—state, liberty, democracy, etc.—has not been closely related to the purposes for which governments exist. At the least, the nature and size of the effort which a society must make, and the physical tools available for the purpose, must influence the degree of effective control exerted by a government over the members of that society. The need to hunt in bands, or defend a settled community against nomads, or irrigate a great desert, will enormously influence the political organization of a community. With Plato as their example, the political philosophers for millennia took as given the structure of communal priorities, and superimposed upon it their political words, which were considered to have an absolute, transcendental content. Political systems rose by analogy, like Chinese philosophies—there was a "body of society," with the king as its head; or the state was a big patriarchal family, with the king as father, or a whale, or the result of a businesslike contract between the rulers and the ruled. Even Tocqueville was prepared to believe that the form of government made the society; not until Marx did the tide turn, and political science become behavioral rather than idealist in orientation.

By then, however, remarkable things had happened. With the spread of literacy and political consciousness, the "concepts" of political science, the Platonic abstractions, had acquired a roughly defined but real experiential content—and a high order of emotional power. Men have died (and, worse, have killed other men) to preserve or to win the words of political science. The question is still enormously tricky, and loaded with pious hypocrisy. The rather admirable if naïve pamphlet resulting from the Williamstown Workshop ("A Program for Improving Bill of Rights Teaching in High Schools," published in the fall of 1962 under the auspices

62

of the Civil Liberties Educational Foundation) proposed "Americans enjoy equality before the law" as one of three "fundamental rights," and "Responsibility means obeying the law" as part of one of four "major concepts." The reader could scarcely gather from this presentation that the workshop participants were referring to that law which, as Anatole France put it, equally forbids rich and poor to sleep under the bridges. Yet there is enough meaning in this ideal of "equality before the law" to make it the first point of attack by the rising anger of the Negro middle class. The structure of a number of societies, especially our own, has been deeply marked by the abstractions of political theory.

Political science can be defined, for teaching, as the study of how such abstractions acquire content, how the content changes, and how the ideal influences the institutions and processes and even purposes of a society. None of this implies that students should be taught "concepts." Reporting the results of a 1962 summer session, a St. Louis group stressing citizenship education happily noted a boy who had come out of the course saying that he had learned some of "the concepts behind our tradition." Concepts do not lie behind tradition; history lies behind both.

What goes wrong with the Civics approach is not the concentration on institutions, which can be presented to reveal both ideals and history, but the tendency to consider institutions in an ideal state (a consideration followed by weasel worries about the "problem" of our failure to live up to our ideals). Examined for the inherent capacity to generate political institutions, the Constitution has two key sections: the commerce clause and the due process clause, both of which are typically (not always) ignored in school. Institutions are not processes, and they do not necessarily reveal the power structure of a community—indeed, they often conceal it. By the study of what the institutions are and how they have been used in the past, however, students can acquire tools for use in the examination of the present.

For teachers who have not had a chance to pick up more than the

63

teacher's-manual material in political science, Appendix A presents a brief statement, in purely political terms, on the origins of certain key American institutions and attitudes.

THE HOMINOCENTRICS AND THE SOCIOCENTRICS

Yet "the Constitution is what the Supreme Court says it is." The personnel of the House Rules Committee determines the fate of legislation. The President is a "liberal" or a "conservative" or a "middle-of-the-roader," "strong" or "weak." Men, not institutions, move events.

For a generation raised at a time when government was normally conducted under the aegis of enthroned royalty, the question of "sovereignty" seemed vital. Laski found it in the Supreme Court, Corwin in the Presidency. (Most teachers gallantly award it to "the people.") Today the President sits with his hand near a red button; an angry Congress forces the executive office to alter foreign policy; the federal bench can compel states to redistrict their legislatures, but not to extend full rights of citizenship to colored citizens.

As a practical matter, where *does* sovereignty lie? What *is* "sovereignty?" Who cares?

The study of political institutions *per se* has a bad name, and deservedly so. ("I can't tell you who's going to win this election," said a commentator in the days before polling, "until I know who's counting the votes.") Written guarantees are not necessarily worth much, as the Soviet Constitution testifies; one of the Amendments in the American Bill of Rights (assuring the right to bear arms) has been distinguished out of existence. It is all very well to speak of the majesty of the law and the impartiality of the bench, but judges are people, too, and their perceptions of the law will be deeply influenced by psychological and sociological set. What looks like one thing institutionally may be something entirely different in practice: the Congressional investigation, designed to secure information which will form a reality principle for legislation, quickly becomes in the hands of a disgruntled legislator a way to punish people he does not like. Municipalities, legally creatures of the state, may be more significant political entities than states because they represent a more restricted community of interests. The need to finance political machinery, which is independent of government machinery, creates both fear and favor, whatever the documents may say. Most of the time, in a democratic community, there are no majorities which can rule; there are only more or less passionate minorities pressuring each other and trading off their influence. In the Defense Department (no longer here or anywhere else a "War Ministry"), clerks allocate contracts which will determine whether men will keep or lose their livelihood, towns will grow into cities or collapse into villages, corporations will prosper or perish. Constitutionally, there is no such power in the United States government; practically, as President Eisenhower warned in his farewell statement, the military-industrial power center has become the strongest single force in American life.

What might be called the Magruder approach to the study of American government, typical of the better schoolwork in this area (Magruder's Textbook still has no serious rivals), is little more than the distant examination of a tray of broken eggshells. At the end of this perusal, the student does not even know whether he is looking at the remains of a breakfast or the by-product of a successful nesting. An extremely strong case can be made for examining the real *operation* rather than the history or ideal condition of institutions.

But the search for personal motivation and societal role easily reduces to a relatively uninformative muckraking, or at worst a scandalous far-fetch. Anyone (it's a free country) may believe that a legislator's attitude toward a dam will be influenced by what he thought of micturition when a child, or that the upwardly-mobile politician must be a short-term manipulator of private inter-

65

ests rather than a long-run analyst of public needs—but even where cases can be cited to "prove" such propositions, the sample is too small to give the cold comfort of statistical certainty, and it is usually the half case out in the third or fourth sigma which turns out to be really important when the historians get around to looking at the period. Granting that there is infinitely more to government than can be brewed behind the oak of a don's chambers, there remains a descriptive validity to the study of political institutions in historical terms.

Cardozo made eloquent answer, in *The Nature of the Judicial Process,* to those who argued that law is what the judges say it is.

Life [he wrote] may be lived, conduct may be ordered, it *is* lived and ordered, for unnumbered human beings, without bringing them within the field where the law can be misread, unless indeed the misreading be accompanied by conscious abuse of power. Their conduct never touches the borderland, the penumbra, where controversy begins. They go from birth to death, their action restrained at every turn by the power of the state, and not once do they appeal to judges to mark the boundaries between right and wrong. I am unable to withhold the name of law from rules which exercise this compulsion over the fortunes of mankind.

Normal fair procedures are the safeguard of the authority of government and the liberty of the citizen. Students do not need to pass through the fire of current political controversy (which is usually, as shall be argued later, off the point of the real issue) to be purified of inane misunderstanding of procedure. Indeed, the crucial question of procedure is likely to disappear when the class undertakes political debates about what ought to be and why evil men oppose it. Chief Justice Warren recently said that the Bill of Rights could not today command a majority vote of Americans, and a number of people were needlessly shocked. Modern Americans have not lived in a community oppressed by the experiences the Bill of Rights prohibits, and their imaginations are committed

66

elsewhere. To understand the institutions of government, it is necessary to find out where they came from, and what evils they were designed to prevent. A taste of the torture cells of the Star Chamber would quickly reveal even to recalcitrant students the dangers of a procedure which can compel self-incrimination.

Children and adolescents, whose behavior is constantly restrained by authority, live in a world of moral imperatives: they feel guilty when they cheat. At least in public they hate the idea of the criminal who goes free—but plenty of teachable evidence lies behind the aphorism that "hard cases make bad law," and the concept is neither difficult to grasp nor irrelevant to the social sciences. Practical politics strikes them as a dirty business in which they can take no interest, because it lacks "principle." A degree of disrespect for political parties is probably a healthy phenomenon—earlier democracies gained nothing whatever by overdeveloped allegiances to Greens or Blues, Guelphs or Ghibellines—but stern views of "principle" lead to a nasty absolutism which can destroy democratic institutions. Contemporary controversies are scarcely proper material for teaching the role of compromise in government; but the Constitutional Convention, honestly considered, is as fine a case history in compromise as an ardent student could ask.

Loyalty to American institutions is likely to be most securely rooted in those who know the experience and intelligence that went into their creation and adaptation. Arguments for or against institutional change can be made only against a background of past institutional change. (What goes wrong with most revolutions, after all, is that they destroy procedure, the only guarantor for what liberty there was.) The problems of modern government are most easily grasped if the problems of previous government, big and small, are understood. Political science as a discipline may indeed be, as its younger professors insist, the queen of the behavioral sciences, drawing service from assorted princesses. But then—as demonstrated by the excellent work of a Harold Lasswell on the

67

rulers or a Seymour Lipset on those they rule—the life goes out of the study, because there is no longer room for the ordinary or the extraordinary, for normal procedure, or for the figure and the idea which somehow change the world. There are only "laws of human behavior," which in the event turn out not to describe anything very accurately.

For teaching purposes, political science is intimately related to history, the history of events, of changing institutions, and of the ideas these institutions express. Fortunately, the hominocentric political scientist is not necessarily alienated from history; and at this writing Franklin Patterson of Tufts, a follower of Lasswell, is working over the books of Hobbes and Locke to find excerpts suitable for an eighth-grade course which will take Anglo-Saxon political man from the Armada to the American Constitution, under the title "From Subject to Citizen." There is certainly enough skill here; given any luck at all, Patterson's course should be an important contribution.

From the classroom:

In the high-income high school of a city on the border between East and Middle West, a senior class in Problems of Democracy has assembled for a discussion of prejudice, discrimination, and segregation. Up front is the committee of five which has looked into the problem and is prepared to answer questions. The textbook is called *Facing Life's Problems,* and the wall above the blackboard is papered with covers from *Time* Magazine. The teacher is sitting in the rear of the room, smiling.

"How are we going to solve the problem of prejudice?" asks the discussion leader, a thin, confident boy.

"I think it's all scapegoating," comes an answer. "If we can keep people from finding scapegoats, we won't have a problem."

"I think we can solve it by organizing, so people meet each other," tries another.

68

A girl says, "It's really a problem of education."

The leader ventures, "We have all been taught prejudice by our parents."

"That's right," a boy says. "For example, my father used to believe that Catholics thought . . ." and the discussion drifts into religion, with adolescents of three faiths making statements about what their religion taught them to believe—a splendid demonstration of the proposition that Sunday-school instruction is no more effective than most other kinds of instruction. The discussion leader feels something has been lost, and interrupts to bring on the next topic:

"We saw in 1954," he says, "when the Supreme Court enacted an anti-segregation law against the southern states . . ."

But time passes quickly, and there are other examples to be cited. "The Jewish people who dare to live in New England," says one of the members of the committee, "they're just ignored, they aren't part of the community. . . ."

Through it all, the teacher sits and nods and smiles. As the bell is about to ring, she rises, walks to her normal position at the head of the class, thanks the committee for their labors, and closes the period with her message:

"Doesn't it all come back to what we said at the beginning of the course—that democracy isn't perfect? Each generation has its own problems, finds its own way to solve them. Democracy can never be perfect, but we can keep trying to make it so. Hate is something that you have to be taught, but we also try to correct . . ."

At Schenley High School in the shadow of the University of Pittsburgh—and of a racially changing neighborhood—Harry Mavrinac is trying a new approach to the required teaching of the state constitution in ninth grade. He is a blunt, stubby, crew-cut, energetic teacher, who strides up and down a center aisle, listens carefully to what students say and reports back to a curriculum-revision group at the university. Among the ideas he is trying out

69

with this class is a public debate by students on whether or not the Pennsylvania Milk Control Commission shall be abolished. The issue is a real one at this moment in Pennsylvania—the local Scripps-Howard paper has made it a crusade—and it raises in highly satisfactory form all the questions on how state laws and regulations are made. At the same time, it can be approached coldly by the class, because it does not touch the passions of any family in the district. Before students can handle themselves in such a debate, of course, they must know a fair amount about Pennsylvania government and how it got to be the way it is. These children are three years younger, and much less lucky, than the seniors in the Problems of Democracy class:

"Now, a constitution is confined only to governments, right?"

"No."

"Well, give me an example."

"Clubs have constitutions, too."

"That's right. Give me some more. . . ." They do. "It goes back to Hammurabi, right? Now, back in Pennsylvania history, how many other constitutions have we had?"

"Four."

"What does that mean? It means they were inadequate. Why did they have to change the constitution of 1804 in 1830? . . . Why didn't the U.S. Constitution become outmoded? . . . Because the Pennsylvania Constitution had too many limits the U.S. Constitution didn't have. It was too rigid. What would you estimate today would be the percentage of people in this state who live in urban areas?"

A boy knows: "Seventy-three percent. It was ony 35 percent when the last constitution was adopted."

"Good. All right, you've read the constitution now. What does it mean by 'Commonwealth'?"

He draws a blank. "Doesn't mean anything but state, really. There are three other commonwealths—Virginia, Kentucky, Mas-

70

sachusetts. I throw this in as a service, no charge: you'll find it on a standardized test someday. What was your honest opinion of the constitution of the Commonwealth of Pennsylvania?"

A girl says, "I never knew there were so many things you could do, so many things you couldn't."

A boy: "It's out of date. It talks about making new counties. It would be pretty hard to make new counties these days."

Another boy: "Also it says nobody can hold public office who has participated in a duel."

"You liked that, eh?" Mavrinac says. "Did you think it was too long?"

The question had not occurred to the class. He gets some shrugged shoulders, and a tentative "Naw."

"I think it's dull and lengthy," Mavrinac says. "Why do you think we have to read it?"

A boy: "So we know about our state government."

A girl: "So we know how we stand."

"Your rights, eh? Think you might forget some of it? Just think how lucky you are you don't live in Louisiana, where the constitution is two hundred pages long. . . ." Mavrinac turns to the board and writes: *Basic Content of All State Constitutions.*

1. Preamble. "Like a preview of attractions."

2. Declaration of Rights. "Why do you suppose there's a Bill of Rights in all the Constitutions?"

A boy says, "It goes back to Montesquieu and Locke."

"What kind of rights are they talking about?"

No response. "Nat!" says Mavrinac, rather surprisingly. "Natter!" And a boy comes in with, "Natural."

3. General Framework:
   Legislative—Art. II & III
   Executive—IV
   Judicial—V
"What are we talking about here?"

71

A girl says, "Checks and balances."

"Anyone know what that means?"

Silence. Mavrinac writes: *4. Amendments.* "For tomorrow," he says, "read up on the Amendments and how they got there. And come prepared to talk about checks and balances. . . ."

In Portland, Oregon, Robert Rowe, a lean young man with an outthrust jaw, who did graduate work in political science at the University of Chicago and spent the academic year 1960-61 as a John Hay Fellow at Yale, is shepherding his eleventh-grade class in American History through the fifth of the six units into which he divides the course. (Westward Movement, Political Parties, U.S. in Conflict, Industrial Development, Political Thought, Development of Art: "You must understand, these are arbitrary, I chose them myself.") For the purpose of the present unit, a thorough understanding of the Constitution is required, and four members of the class are putting the rest through an oral quiz on what the document says. Rowe sits in the circle with the class, and contributes.

"The first amendment," a boy says, "offers freedom of speech. What are the two exceptions to this?"

A girl says, "Slander and . . ."

Another girl says, "You can't advocate violent overthrow of the government."

Rowe breaks in: "Why do you suppose this has developed? I remember when I went to high school this never came up. What's the reason people in interpreting this amendment have made it different?"

"The Communists."

"Yes."

"What two amendments," asks another boy up front, "support the interpretation that a man's home is his castle?"

"The fourteenth and the fifth."

Rowe says, "The fourteenth and the fifth have something in

72

common—due process of law. Could you tell me what's the difference between the two?"

A girl says, "The fourteenth applies to the states, too."

"Now," Rowe says, "what *is* due process of law?"

A boy says, "According to the laws of the land."

"You got that from the textbook. Let's do better."

"Well, it means what's done is jake with the Constitution, and the laws."

"Done under certain guarantees," Rowe says.

The fifth amendment is explored further, and Rowe intervenes again to check a correct answer. "What is an indictment by a grand jury, Nancy?"

"It's an accusation."

"What would be the comparable thing among executive or judicial offices?"

"Impeachment."

A girl on the committee asks, "What was the basic purpose of the Bill of Rights, and why did they put it in the Constitution?"

Rowe comments, "That's a very good question."

The class struggles for a while, and gets nowhere. The girl who asked the question finally supplies the answer: "They did it to protect the people from the government. . . ."

Not one class in a thousand in the United States could handle this material so well; yet the visitor had been taken by the administration to Rowe's room because he sometimes played the guitar and sang folk songs to the class, and perhaps could be persuaded to do so for the walking delegate from the American Council of Learned Societies. Earlier that same day, another class of bright children in the same city, taught by a man closely involved with the Portland curriculum-reform movement, had wandered aimlessly through a discussion of "loyalty" and the flag-salute cases, as though the doctrine of judicial review did not exist. The exasperated visitor had finally pointed out to an argumentative trio of students

73

that the Bill of Rights had been written to tell them as the majority what they could not do, and a murmur of outrage went through the class. "I think that's wrong," a boy said vigorously. "I think the majority should be able to do what it wants to do." To the answer that such an attitude was his privilege, but was not in fact the current American system, he replied, "I don't care."

TEACHING

On his way to a school in a low-lying district of Elkhart, Indiana, the economist Lawrence Senesh of Purdue noticed that the streets were filthy. He proposed to a class of third-graders that each of them bring in the trash that was in his path on his way from home to school; to the principal's horror, it filled a corridor. Under the joint guidance of Senesh and their teacher, the third-graders picked apart the garbage and analyzed why it was there. Three main sources of filth were identified:

1. Dirt made by the people who lived in the neighborhood, especially the children. Neighborhood action could take care of that, and the children pledged themselves to watch their own habits and agitate among their friends and families.

2. Dirt from the unpaved road beside the railroad tracks, and from periodic discharges of the sewer system, which lies uncomfortably near the ground in this district. The neighborhood could do little about that; it was a city problem. Pressure should be put on the city government.

3. Dirt left from the spring overflow of the little river that runs near the school. Here even the city couldn't help much, because the river had its source far away. Even the state might not be big enough, because the river ran through more than one state.

Senesh, who had been working with these children in economics only, decided the time had come to teach some political science. . . .

The elements of political socialization are all around the child

74

from an early age. All games require rules, and the people in the game must "play fair." There are laws for the home, laws for the classroom, laws for the playground. (Laws for grownups, too; Daddy must stop the car at the red light.) Most schools give children a taste of election procedure from an early age, with class presidents, milk monitors, pencil sharpeners, etc. Almost any group of children will throw forth a leadership, based perhaps on physical strength or abounding energy, pleasantness of manner or the cleverness to know "how you make it" in school surroundings. Some of these situations do in fact relate to the more formal institutions of government, some do not. Most political scientists hate school elections, on any level up to and including student government at the colleges, because the schools are always rigging the situation; students know perfectly well that the purpose of student government is to serve the needs of the administration. Yet in the real world, too, the power of elected governments is circumscribed by more potent governments or by the situation of the community which does the electing. Unfortunately, to the participant in political activity, each roll of the dice is unique: the results rather than the procedure, the story rather than the moral, remain to be learned from the experience. This difficulty—that the story must be bright enough to build interest, but not so brilliant that it shadows its own point—is common to teaching, forensics, advertising, and most other forms of purposeful communication. Political science suffers worst of all.

History is intrinsically messy; social sciences are intrinsically neat. The interrelationship of custom and law is a prime topic in political science, and the American experience with prohibition is an excellent case in point; but if the teacher hopes to get across any serious notion of what he is talking about, he must avoid "the Jazz Age" at all costs. Edwin Fenton of Carnegie Tech used prohibition as one of three cases in a unit of this sort; the other two were the FEPC in Pittsburgh and the Russian attempt to eliminate the family as a major economic and political unit in Soviet society.

The change in the relative importance of the Security Council and General Assembly of the United Nations could also be used interestingly in this connection. Yet there are also cases when a law that seems to go completely against the community grain becomes effective immediately, because it expresses a widespread desire to get rid of a custom. Perhaps the most obvious example of this phenomenon in recent years was the prohibition of horn honking in Paris; in a single day, the characteristic bleating sound of the city vanished entirely. Most American children and adolescents, even the itsy-bitsy Birchers, believe that the government can do anything; and also that "you can't change human nature." One of the purposes of instruction in political science, whatever the "goal" of the teacher, must be to put juice into slogans like Bismarck's aphorism that politics is the art of the possible and Hugo's pronouncement about the power of an idea whose time has come. If such purposes are to be achieved, examples must be carefully chosen for relevance rather than for apparent importance.

Two sets of case studies in current politics, one from the Eagleton Foundation at Rutgers, the other from the University of Alabama via Ford, are available for use in the high schools. Neither is wholly satisfactory for teaching purposes, though many of the Eagleton pamphlets make fascinating reading and their emphasis on local issues in individual American cities and states limits the dangers of irrelevance in discussion. Both sets of pamphlets are essentially behavioral in their approach to political science, which means (to be nasty) that personalities often overwhelm the issue. Yet an intelligent teacher—like Gordon Neisser of Watchung Hills Regional High School in northern New Jersey (now of the Harvard School of Education)—can unquestionably use them to teach the institutional framework within which the case occurred.

Despite a certain sickly conventionality, the Grass Roots Guides of the Center for Information on America set forth information in an orderly manner and ought to be used more than they are; none

76

of them completely ignores the historical background of government. George Probst's recordings based on Tocqueville's *Democracy in America* deal romantically but informatively with the sea change in American institutions at the time of Jackson. The textbooks, by and large, are niggling and light on ideas, and the films about American government—one excepts Peter Odegard's glamorous but slapdash television course, which is honest enough—are the worst sort of romantic propaganda. Local history is rarely used for teaching political science, even in the Civics courses. As one might expect in a field of study with so long a history, many of the most valuable readings are old. A really careful selection can be made, however, only on empirical evidence—by trying out the material, and attempting to find out how much children *use* it. Government documents and committee reports, with their inevitable emphasis on "big problems," should be avoided on grounds of style, probity, and utility.

Most political scientists seem to feel that their field can be handled through history courses, provided the history teachers know what they are doing. By and large, they would be willing to give up the Civics course (universally despised, though it was launched originally by a university political scientist, Charles Merriman of Harvard). For the last few years, the American Political Science Association has taken a booth and sold subscriptions to its journal at the annual convention of the National Council for the Social Studies. No further action by the association or its leading members seems in prospect just now, though there are flurries of interest below the surface of inactivity.

A behaviorist minority of political scientists chafes under the restraints of history—but has not yet offered anything in its place, except some ideas for improving the hopeless Problems course. Most such political scientists feel a first love for government and political action in the big world; and most of the more scholarly remainder are so engaged in exploring the irrational roots of politi-

77

cal behavior that they cannot easily shift to filling in the historical and ideational lacks of students. (They know all about such things; therefore, obviously, students know about them, too. Repeated shocks in the college classroom produce only irritable condemnation of the schools.) This observer doubts that the behavioral political scientists should be encouraged to interest themselves in schools. Political Man is as dead as Economic Man; yet he is necessary pedagogically, if only because the old belief in his existence explains the persistent forms of the procedural structure. And without him, at present, the political scientist has no way to control the introduction of irrelevance in teaching. The purpose of teaching is not to peddle Truth but to stimulate disciplined ideas. More than anyone else, perhaps, the behavioral political scientist needs what the history teachers call the courage to exclude.

ECONOMICS

From the classroom:

For most of this term at the Hawthorne School in Elkhart, Indiana, Mrs. Esther Oyer's first grade has been picking its way around the debris of building repairs and additions. Because Elkhart, under the leadership of Purdue's Lawrence Senesh, is engaged in a serious attempt to teach economics on the elementary-school level, the class is doing something with the construction besides throwing the loose bricks. On a table near the front of the classroom is a display: bricks, sand, and mortar labeled "materials," a big carpenter's level, a trowel, and a hammer labeled "tools," and drawings of men at work labeled "labor." These exhibits are shown and explained to the visitor, and Mrs. Oyer says to the class, "Are these all the tools?"

"No," a boy says. "There are big tools, too."

"What kind of big tools?"

"Hoist . . . steam shovel . . . mixers . . ."

78

"We learned," Mrs. Oyer explains, "a lot of new words." To the class: "Do the bricklayers own the big tools?"

"No," another boy says. "The company owns them."

On the rear wall there is a display, divided into two parts. "Families Buy Some Things for Themselves—Food, Books, Clothing, Furniture, Cars, Homes, Pets, Toys" (Each with a picture; the picture of the book has words written on it: "Dick and Jane, and Sally and Tim and Spot and Puff.") The other side reads: "Families Buy Some Things All Together—Bridges, Parks, Policemen, Schools, Sidewalks, Firemen, Roads."

"What did the men get for working on our school?"

"They got money income."

"What did they spend the money for?"

. . . Along one of the walls there is an "experience chart," as follows:

WHY OUR FATHERS CHOSE THEIR JOBS

Because he likes the work
Because a man asked him
Because he couldn't find any other one
Because he was needed
Because he was trained at school
Because he was laid off his first job
Because he can earn more money
Because when he got out of the Army it was the only job open . . .

"If a man wanted to buy the big tools," Mrs. Oyer says, "how would he do it?"

"He could borrow the money," a boy says.

"Where would he borrow it?"

"From a bank."

"Where did the bank get it from?"

"People's savings," says another boy—"and he'd have to pay it back."

Yet another boy says, "He'd have to pay back *more*."

79

"That's right," says the teacher.

"Interest," says the boy.

The class is now gathered into a semicircle before the blackboard, and Mrs. Oyer moves on to new material. "Could you think of anyone who's not working, and could you tell me why?"

A girl: "My grandmother, because she's crippled."

A boy: "My neighbor, because he's retired. He's this friend of mine, he's eighty-seven."

A girl: "My great-grandma's ninety, but she keeps trying."

A few more examples of great age are given, and then a girl tires a new tack: "My mommy doesn't work because of the baby."

Another girl: "My mommy doesn't work because the brother makes all that mess, she has to clean it up."

To Mrs. Oyer's regret (but not her despair), the necessary information won't come. She turns to the board and says, "People who are working are [she writes the word] *employed*." The class reads the word. "Now, what do we call someone who is *not* employed?"

There is a brief delay; then a boy ventures, timidly, "Unemployed?"

"That's right. Now, tonight, we are all going to think of a person who is unemployed, and we'll talk about it tomorrow. . . ."

In Elkhart's Beardsley School, a newer building in a neighborhood of newer homes, Miss Marguerite Roderick is taking her second grade through a unit on the neighborhoods where people live and work. "Now, what sort of neighborhood do you live in?"

A girl says, "Suburban—it's new, it's clean, it has very few stores."

Another girl mutters, "Residential."

A boy says, "Commercial—there's lots of stores and hobby shops, bargain shops, doctors, laundromats . . ."

"Does anybody know another neighborhood? Gail?"

"There's lots of factories. Industrial."

80

"What industry do we have near our school?"

A boy says, "Conn."

"And what do Conn's make?"

"Instruments."

"What word could we have used instead of 'make'?"

"Produce."

"And what do we call producers?"

"Manufacturers.'"

"Now, what kind of neighborhood did we say we were going to talk about today?"

And the class choruses: "Rural!"

Miss Roderick, a tall girl with a casual manner, grins at her charges. "Sometimes we say 'Country.' Well, you remember Mr. Brown. A very unfortunate thing happened to him."

A girl says, "He was injured by his corn picker."

"Yes. First, we discussed whether he was smart to buy a corn picker, or whether he should have hired a number of men instead. What did we decide?"

"We decided he was right to buy the corn picker."

"Yes," says Miss Roderick thoughtfully. "Today, let's talk about risk. Since we're in the country, does Farmer Brown have any risks besides injury?"

The class is stuck briefly on machinery, the corn picker to the front of everyone's mind, but finally a boy says, "If he didn't pick his crop at the right time of year it would rot," and the class goes into the luck of the weather and its influence on the farmer's profits.

The class is alert, intelligent, moving well; and Miss Roderick takes a gamble. "Now," she says, "let's suppose the weather is just right, and Farmer Brown has a great big beautiful crop. Do you think the other farmers all around him had a great big beautiful crop, too?"

"Sure."

"So everybody has a great big beautiful crop. Do people *want*

81

that much corn? Is Farmer Brown going to be able to *sell* it? And if he does sell it, what kind of price is he going to get?"

There are hands up around the class, but Miss Roderick is aiming for more than an answer. "Milk time!" she calls cheerily, and disperses the class. "You think about that until tomorrow."

As the class moves off in groups to pick up its milk containers, the little boys and girls are arguing with each other, in the manner of college students at a good college, about how well Farmer Brown is going to do with his great big beautiful crop. Break your heart.

At Elkhart's Lincoln School, Melba Lauber's third grade is going over local industries, why they are here and how they work. A beginning teacher, Miss Lauber dresses for school as she would for an office, in a stylish apricot dress and spike-heeled shoes. Children (and visitors) like pretty girls; her appearance and her energy more than make up for any lack of experience. She is at the board, going over, in Senesh's way, what might otherwise be labeled "the factors of production."

"What does a factory need?" Miss Lauber asks, and writes on the board the called responses from the class:

"Energy."

"Equipment."

"Land and buildings."

"The workers."

"And the man with the idea."

"They have to have savings."

Miss Lauber turns around. "Where are the savings, Pam?"

"In the bank."

"What else do they need, Mike?"

"Transportation."

"Customers."

A boy says, "You have to have engineers."

"Yes, and that goes in with 'workers.'"

82

"Profit."

"Anything else? No? Well, that's pretty good. But you forgot"—and she writes on the board on her own initiative—"materials."

The meat of the class is the teacher's description of her recent visit to Richardson's, a trailer manufacturer not far from the school. "They make pre-fab trailers—one every seventeen minutes!" She passes around the pictures Richardson's had given her for her class ("Yes, to keep!"), and describes the trailers. "The man said they cost about four thousand or five thousand dollars. How much does a house cost? . . . They use a lot of hand tools at Richardson's—can you think why? . . . Richardson's has 250 workers, and 189 of them help put the trailers together. The man at Richardson's told me that 150 of the 189 are really skilled workers.

"I asked him where they learned their skills. He said that some had learned at other trailer factories, and some had learned here. You know, back in the old days, Elkhart had a buggy industry, with lots of skilled carpenters. Some people think that's why we have so many skilled workers now. Now, where do Richardson's get their materials? Can you guess?"

One boy says, "Michigan."

Another says, "Right here in Elkhart."

"That's right. They buy their wood from the Elkhart Saw Mill. . . ."

The magnificent honesty of the Elkhart program is essentially the creation of Lawrence Senesh himself, a short, stout, tough-minded, enthusiastic Hungarian with long gray hair and endless energy. He arrived in this country shortly before the war and worked in a lumber yard before enlisting in the Army. Capitalizing on the GI Bill, he studied at the University of Denver, then stayed to help set up a School of Creative Graphics, art being his first love. He did graduate work at the London School of Economics, and signed on in the early days for the Joint Council on Economic

83

Education, which recommended him for his chair at Purdue. Since 1958, he has worked at Elkhart two and three days a week—driving ninety miles each way, teaching teachers and taking over classes to learn and then to demonstrate what can be done. He could not have managed the enormous problems of what he was attempting without the support of the Elkhart superintendency (and $10,000 to $25,000 a year, mostly from local business); and Ann McAllister, Elkhart's supervisor of elementary education, has given at least as much time as Senesh himself to making sure that teachers know what they are doing with the material Senesh provides. But the good proportion of success in Elkhart schools—and all fourteen elementary schools are involved in the Senesh program—is a tribute to Senesh's imagination and intellectual fierceness, and to his control over what is done, a control given to him willingly by teachers who feel their own powers rising with the power of effective teaching ideas.

Elkhart's economics program is as much an oddity in American education as the Junior Archeological Society of Baton Rouge. Attempts to imitate it, in Indianapolis and in the Greater Cleveland Social Studies Project, have failed completely, because the people supervising the work did not realize how different Senesh's program was from the usual elementary curriculum (in Cleveland, for example, much of the early material deals with stores, because stores look simple to teachers; nobody had noticed that Senesh had omitted stores almost completely, or knew enough economics to understand that retailing is one of the most complicated and difficult topics in the field). But surely a strong idea need not remain an educational oddity.

ECONOMIC ILLITERACY

Economics as a school subject has a long history; as early as 1894, the Committee of Ten on the secondary-school curriculum was recommending that it should not be taught. Yet students come into contact constantly with economic institutions, from the allowance and the corner drugstore to the spare-time job and the taxes withheld from the salary. Children receive, handle, and spend money from an early age; family activity is quite obviously influenced by income; and the father's source of income is a matter of importance from an early age. The texture of life is inevitably a function, in part, of economic activity: "Getting and spending, we lay waste our powers." And, of course, the great national rivalry with the Russians is superficially explained, by both parties, in terms of economic organization and accomplishment.

As an academic study, however, economics is fairly recent; even as a branch of philosophy, political economy cannot be traced back much before the early eighteenth century. It is generally and erroneously believed to have started with Adam Smith ("who was," the late Joseph Schumpeter used to say, "a very dull and pedantic man. He loomed so large because nobody ever looked behind him. All the dull and pedantic professors of economics would read Adam Smith and say, 'How wonderful! How profound! I always thought so myself.'"). The study of economics is almost certainly a byproduct of the growth of capitalism, which drastically changed the relations of persons in the body politic, and demanded explanation. Though there are important French contributions as early as 1800, the field was dominated by Englishmen until the late nineteenth century. Marx drew virtually all his evidence from the English scene, and virtually all his economic theory from English economists (particularly Ricardo). It is important to note that Marx was an original theorist in history, not in economics; men like Jevons and Marshall were far more interesting and imaginative economists than Marx. Economics is a discipline; not everything that deals with economic topics can be regarded as "economics."

Of the social sciences, economics was the first to lay claim to "scientific" status. From the beginning, economists induced "laws" from observed experience of their contemporaries. Starting with Cournot, and gathering power with Jevons, Marshall, Walras,

Barone, and Fisher, economists applied mathematics (especially the calculus) to the derivation and extrapolation of these laws. Nevertheless, it can fairly be said that the dominant body of economic theory at any period is closely related to the election returns. The spread of colonies created mercantilism; the growth of private industry promoted *laissez-faire*; welfarism and dread of the business cycle have established neo-Keynesian macro-economics, an emphasis on government rather than on private activity, and a chef's rather than a diner's attitude toward the porridge of statistics.

By and large, the schools have been impervious to the flow of economic doctrine. Economics courses in high schools, until recently, dealt almost exclusively with the part of the iceberg that shows. On the bottom level of utilitarian education, economics was reduced to persuading students to read a scale in a meat market and to multiply monthly payments by twelve or twenty-four to find the price of something purchased on an installment plan. Where efforts have been made to develop something more interesting, emphasis has been mostly on institutions—money and the banking system, the stock market, farming, corporations, labor unions, government, etc. Equilibrium occurs on balance sheets. Little attempt has been made on the high-school level to teach the economic frame of reference, the search for interrelationships and causal factors in economic motion.

Most students have no economics at all, though it is now estimated that as many as a quarter of current high-school graduates have been exposed to a semester course called "economics.'" The activities of elementary and junior-high classes—visiting banks and milk bottleries, simulating stock-market investments or launching little businesses—make no approach whatever to economic analysis. "Problems" courses are if anything more misleading in this area than in others, because they deliberately conceal the interrelations that are the essence of analysis. And a study of history, though indispensable for the avoidance of analytical solecism, will not by itself produce the habit of mind which is at the bottom of economics. It is scarcely surprising that students are still "economic illiterates," to use the popular new phrase, when they emerge from high school.

Different people are upset by different facets of this illiteracy. The businessman worries about surveys which show that most Americans believe average profits to be between a sixth and a third of gross sales. He agonizes over the nation's obvious failure to understand the contribution of capital and management to productivity. He despairs about the prevailing national assumption that appropriate government action is a sovereign cure for economic ills. And the stock market gives him cold sweats. He is only too willing to pay for economic education.

The economist, on the other hand, is troubled when an eminent U.S. Senator and an almost equally eminent New York newspaper columnist find grave national danger in the fact that accumulated indebtedness in the United States has passed the one-trillion-dollar mark—as though people could get interest on their savings, or buy meaningful life insurance, if other people and governments were not willing to "go into debt" by borrowing the money to build factories and houses, schools and dams. The economist is concerned when commentators proclaim that our Latin American aid programs are menaced by a lack of democracy down South, ignoring catastrophic drops in commodity prices and our neighbors' ugly tendencies to export their capital to Europe instead of using it at home. He is appalled when people object to the oilman's depletion allowance on the moralistic grounds that it rewards fat cats rather than on the realistic grounds that it channels what seems a disproportionately large share of the national economic effort to the search for petroleum. He is irritated when a business writes off capital investment more quickly for tax purposes, then complains about a "drop in profits" because bookkeepers have shifted ledger figures from "profits" to "depreciation." Headlines about the stock exchanges are

87

for the economist the last straw: to him, a stock exchange is only a mechanism, a place where people swap pieces of paper that influence capital creation only through their effect on the entirely separate market for new securities.

And all the complaints, the businessman's worries and the economist's irritation, are rather confusing to the educator who is expected to cope with the illiteracy. He honestly thought he was teaching economics all along, when he showed children how to open a bank account or get a social security card, when he uttered the magic words "Industrial Revolution" to a history class, when he marked students wrong on an examination if they did not know that there are twelve member banks in the Federal Reserve System. The agitation about "economic illiteracy" has brought home to an increasing number of teachers the disturbing fact that they are economically illiterate themselves. Sarcely any of them majored in economics in college; only half the social studies staff had as much as a single year of college economics. That introductory economics course, moreover, is probably, against severe competition, the nearest approach to a total waste of time to be found in the colleges. (Yale, which is trying to take economics seriously, recently dropped the introductory course as a requirement for concentration in the field, leaving it to plague only those who need credits for "general education.") In no other subject area do teachers know so little about what they are teaching; and, to compound the problem, there is painfully little recent material in economics which can honestly be recommended—on grounds of content, style, or clarity of thought —to teachers or to students. "Economists," says James Calderwood of Southern California, who has been trying to turn out more useful materials, "still want to write for each other."

From the classroom:

In a West Coast city, the teacher in charge of revising the economics unit in a Problems course is putting a class of high-school seniors through their paces in money and banking. She is gray, brisk, tough, enormously confident, and spectacularly ignorant. On the board the twelve Federal Reserve districts are listed, with the sub-branches under the names of the member banks. The teacher is waving a five-dollar bill, borrowed from a student.

"This is what we call 'elastic currency.' How does the government put this money into circulation? I'll tell you. I'm a banker, and I want to make loans—but I don't have any money. So I take my notes to the Fed as collateral, and they lend money to me, they print this five-dollar bill. I lend it to you. When you pay me back, I take it back to the Fed and redeem my note, and the five-dollar bill disappears. . . . The one-dollar silver certificate is backed by round silver dollars, one for each certificate. It's backed by value. This five-dollar bill, what's back of it is gold, government bonds, discounted notes, and bank reserves. It didn't exist until I loaned it. . . .

"Anything you take out of the land, you have to pay the government a 'severance tax.' I don't care if it's gold, coal, timber, copper —you have to pay a tax. . . .

"When the British nationalized, they didn't pay for it. They said to people, 'Your great-grandfather got all of the money out of this that he paid for it, and it's not his any more, and we're taking it. . . .'"

"The Board of Governors of the Federal Reserve System is appointed by the President of the United States with an eye to representing all the interests in the United States—farmers, big business, labor. . . .

"The National Banks gave the government a hold on bank loans. These banks were permitted to print money if they deposited gold in the Treasury. Very few of these notes are still in existence, because the power to tax is the power to destroy and the government taxed these notes heavily. . . ."

Later the visitor is accorded an interview with this teacher, and, struggling for questions, inquires how she stimulates students' interest in economics. "Well," she says, "I begin by telling them that economics can be divided into two kinds, macro and micro, and that arouses their interest right away, of course. . . ."

In a wealthy Los Angeles suburb, a class of seniors, with an average IQ around 120, is taking a term's worth of economics. Their text is Goodman-Moore, *Today's Economics,* which the Tulsa school system regards as somewhat elementary for better-than-average ninth graders. The teacher wanted Augustus Smith's *Economics for Our Time,* which is somewhat less trivial, but, he says, "the board didn't like Smith's use of the words 'social democracy.' " College texts cannot be used because they are not on the state-approved list for high schools.

One wonders, however, how much difference a text would make, because the tone of any course must be set in the classroom; and in this classroom much use is made of "resource persons" who do not know any economics. Today's resource person is a representative of the Social Security administration, and the twenty big, bright adolescents in the class sit with glazed eyes as he reveals the marvels of social security:

"You may wonder why you have to get a number. Well, if your card had just your name on it, it might get scrambled with the cards of people who had names like yours. Your name might be Bear, and there would be other people who spelled Bear just the way you do. There might even be somebody else named Harry Bear. So we have a numbering system . . ."

In a wealthy New York suburb, a class of seniors, with an average IQ around 120, is taking a term's worth of economics. The text here is Augustus Smith, but the basic reading is Soule's *Ideas of the Great Economists* and Heilbroner's *The Worldly Philosophers.* A gangling boy is reading a report on Thorstein Veblen:

"I don't know," he begins, "how many of you have read Heilbroner's chapter—"

90

A voice from the floor calls, "Take a guess."

"Well, I'll summarize it. . . .

"America was different from the economy of Europe, where money, no matter how much of it you might have, didn't determine your social status. . . . When one of these great robber barons like J. Pierpont Morgan committed some great injustice to get more money, nobody thought it was anything unusual, or there was anything wrong with it. . . .

"Veblen's flaw was that he was not quite able to see that a democratic society could correct its own excesses. The reason he couldn't see it is that he was the product of his age, the age of the robber barons, when businessmen were interested in making profits rather than producing goods. . . ."

At the end the teacher, a young man in rather good tweeds, takes over: "Somebody said that a democratic capitalist economy such as ours has merely made the vices of the rich available to the poor. . . . In World War II we ran a Veblenesque economy. We called in the experts. There was no unemployment. We controlled profits—they were adequate, of course—we rationed everything, and we accomplished miracles of production. . . .

"Veblen's contribution was that he destroyed Economic Man. He insisted that man could make rational decisions, wasn't just pushed around by economic forces. . . ."

At the end of the period, the visitor asked the teacher where he had studied his economics. The teacher, an intelligent man, nodded his head and grinned. "My master's," he said, "is in English."

"I know," said the visitor, sympathetically.

"Yes," said the teacher.

A PORTRAIT OF THE REFORM MOVEMENT AS A FAILURE

The first decently financed postwar effort to reform school instruction in a subject area was started in economics in 1949, when

91

G. Derwood Baker of New York University founded the Joint Council for Economic Education. In the years since, several millions of dollars (no firm estimate can be made) have been spent on activities sponsored by or related to the Joint Council and its forty-three state and local affiliates. Except in Elkhart and perhaps in Tulsa, the results of the expenditure are virtually invisible.

Many reasons, from questions of personality to the "controversial" nature of the material, can be adduced for the ineffectiveness of the Joint Council in its first thirteen years. Two factors, however, seem to be central—the refusal of the economists to become involved with the actual teaching of their subject, and the insistence on an unfortunate "goal." Both are still in operation.

The "Joint" in the Council was seen from the beginning as a meeting of economists and educators. The obvious *modus vivendi* was to assume that the economists knew about the economics and the educators, once they were informed, would know how to teach it. Compromise was the order of the day. Unfortunately, the educators were not conscious of how little economics they knew, and the economists suffered a gloomy understanding of how little they knew about teaching. The economists sat still while the Joint Council encouraged aimless visits to supermarkets, mock corporations for juniors, household budgets, "business arithmetic," even the teaching of economics through literature (lists of allegedly appropriate novels were developed at a summer workshop at the University of Vermont). Much stress was placed on "initiatory activities, developmental activities and culminating activities." Among the latter, recommended in one Joint Council booklet, were "Have a classroom radio quiz program. . . . Arrange a model Junior Town meeting. . . . Make a scrap book containing the clippings brought in by the class. . . . Write a short play with brief scenes to summarize several of the highlights of the topic. . . . Review the purposes of this unit as drawn up at the beginning of the study, and try to decide to what extent these purposes have been accomplished. Discuss, also, the kinds of attitude changes which students

92

have experienced as a result of this study." No serious study of economics could possibly lead to such culminations, which would seem trivial beside the content, but the economists never rebelled.

Except for a few film strips, the Joint Council did not attempt on a national basis to develop new teaching materials and train teachers specifically to use them. ("Our position," says director Moe Frankel, "is not to create material for kids, but to create demand and let the publishers provide material.") The division of labor in the council prevented either party from considering the notion that teaching ideas must grow out of profound knowledge of what is to be taught. Moreover, because the council sought influence, most of the participating educators came from higher political echelons in school systems, colleges of education, Councils for the Social Studies, etc. The economists rarely received a chance to choose the teachers with whom they would work, and educational bureaucrats were always at liberty to decide how much of what the economists gave them they wished to communicate down to the hewers of wood and drawers of water in their classrooms.

These principles of operation were accepted by the National Task Force on Economic Education, appointed in May, 1960, by the American Economics Association, at the request of the Committee for Economic Development. Indeed, the five eminent economists in the Task Force were told not only to avoid any suggestions about how the economics they required could be taught, but to ignore the problem of materials for students to read, which were to be chosen by another, less eminent, wholly separate committee. The unreality of the Task Force report traces partly to the irresponsibility of this assignment.

One local Joint Council effort, in Oklahoma, did produce something for students to read—a pamphlet entitled *Cowboys, Cattle and Commerce,* written for the Tulsa school system by the economic historian Jim E. Reese of Oklahoma University. Reese and Harold Bienvenu, now of Los Angeles State College, sat down together and thought about the teaching of ninth-grade economics. "We

93

agreed," Reese recalls, "that the usual principles course is no good on the college level, and there could be no justification for writing it down for ninth-graders. We decided we would take an industry, and see how much economics we could teach from one industry. We took cattle because of the TV programs, and because it was Tulsa. Then we asked what we wanted ninth graders to know, and we decided the important things were the market economy, prices, and the interactions of the two. We started writing with a committee of fourteen, one teacher from each of the Tulsa junior high schools, and then we got it down to the five teachers we wanted to work with. When we were finished, we were afraid not only that students wouldn't get it, but that *teachers* wouldn't get it. We wrote a teacher's guide three times as long as the pamphlet, and had an eight-week in-service training program, every Wednesday night for two hours, specifically on how to teach the economics contained in the pamphlet."

Even this procedure wasn't enough; apparently there are only a handful of Tulsa teachers who understand the quality of the tool Reese placed in their hands. But the pamphlet remains, and could be used on the junior-high level anywhere in the country. Moe Frankel, who taught at Scott High School in East Orange before he became director of the Joint Council, knows that it is the most valuable item in his stock, and quietly tries to promote it, with little success.

The originality of *Cowboys, Cattle and Commerce* had little influence on most of the economists and educators in the Joint Council because they were looking to reach much bigger objectives. Ben W. Lewis of Oberlin, the man most responsible for pushing the American Economics Association into the Task Force effort, made the argument in a speech in 1956:

The case for economics in the schools is made of the same stuff as the case for democracy itself. The logic is inexorable, and its import in today's situation is alarming. Democracy—and this we have on the very highest authority—means government by the people. But the affairs of government, in large and increasing measure, are economic affairs. ... The stakes, to put the matter bluntly, are the survival of democracy and human freedom. Freedom will not remain if democracy expires, and democracy will not last beyond the day when it fails to discharge the political-economic tasks which we ask it to perform. . . . We are "the people" on whose economic understanding and economic sense the outcome of our epic adventure in self-government rests.

Lewis was a member of the Task Force, and the opening page of its report is a paraphrase of his speech. The assignment accepted by the Task Force was to determine "the economic understanding . . . needed for good citizenship." This approach is immediately disabling to any teaching effort, because it reduces inquiry to technology—and to a technology where the tools cannot be tried by the students. ("We are getting away," Edwin Nourse told a Joint Council meeting, "from the natural science concept of economics, with its proscription of value judgments. We are moving over to the social science concern about motives and incentives. . . . Social science emphasizes value concepts or ideals as defining ends toward which we shall use the methods of science to devise effective means.") Its essential falsity is easily apparent to students, if not always to teachers.

Nobody but a social scientist or a government analyst has to know much economics to play his societal role properly. Adam Smith argued that an invisible hand worked in the marketplace to assure that people following their own simple, unenlightened self-interest would in fact promote the common good. Though matters never worked out precisely the way Smith thought they would, it is still true in capitalist, semi-capitalist, and even some state-capitalist countries that the play of market prices heavily influences the allocation of resources to one sort of product rather than another (which is what the study of economics is all about). The business-man's natural search for profit and the worker's natural search for

95

higher wages are still vital elements in the progress of the economy; and neither party has to know any economics to fulfill his function. The late Joseph Schumpeter once said that a businessman did not need to know economics any more than a gourmet at a great restaurant needed to know how his intestines functioned.

Miracles of economic education are not going to help the cause of "citizenship." Almost everyone has real economic interests which can be served or harmed by government action, and existing pressure groups do, in fact, represent the economic interests of their constituents. Thoughtful farmers probably do not believe that current federal agricultural policies help the national economy, but nobody doubts that they help the farmer. An understanding of the doctrine of optimum allocation will not make the farmer cease his quest for price supports, any more than an understanding of the doctrine of comparative advantage will make the textile manufacturer welcome competition from Hong Kong. Senators and Congressmen will continue to pressure the government to locate a defense establishment or a veterans' hospital or a harbor improvement in their territory rather than in less costly or more convenient territories, however much economics the public has learned. And "selfish interests," despite what gets said by the advocates of "citizenship," are not necessarily harmful to the progress of democracy. The balances struck in a plural society, where local and occupational and small-group interests rank higher than social-class or "national" interests, are likely to promote peaceful adjustments to change in a way that rigid adherence to economic logic might not.

Anything anybody wants to teach can be defended as necessary for "good citizenship." James Bryant Conant once insisted that literature should be taught because it promoted citizenship; the Modern Language Association argues that in this age of jet transport foreign languages are needed for citizenship; scientists say that we need citizens informed of the capabilities and limitations of science. Concentration on the public-policy aspects of study, however, tends to distort the nature of what is studied, because public policy in any field has meaning *only* through its impact on private choice. Insistence on the predominance of public policy also gets educators into unnecessary trouble by injecting political problems into even the most elementary aspects of a subject.

What people need, for both personal and political reasons, is some way of organizing the events around them to make sense of a highly complicated world. Economics, properly understood, is not a "body of knowledge"; it is a habit of mind, which enables people to select what is relevant to the how and why of changes in production and consumption, income and employment, interest, rent and taxes. Lacking this habit of mind, Americans are prone to conspiracy theories, peaks of excitement and pits of despair, blockbuster solutions for surgical problems. Economic illiteracy probably *is* some small danger to democracy, but only because it raises the decibel count of the debate, thereby slightly increasing the chance that the minority will refuse to lose, or the majority will push the losers too hard.

The argument that something should be studied for reasons of "citizenship," however, is simply an assertion of self-importance by the proprietors of the subject. Even more self-seeking is the Task Force argument that "the development of economic understanding involves first and above all the capacity to think *rationally*"—an argument which carries with it the clear implication that *we* are rational and the rest of you bums are not. In point of fact, economists seem to have a somewhat greater ego involvement in their theories than any scholastics except the sociologists; and historically, of course, one can easily trace the rise of economic arguments to the societal and personal situations of their authors—though the argument may remain important long after its causes have disappeared.

"Rationality" to an economist invariably means the promotion of "economic growth" and efficiency. Thus the members of the

97

Task Force apply their reason to "the many heated arguments about tariffs. . . . To employers and workers in an industry threatened by foreign competition, personal goals are likely to be paramount. Workers want most of all to keep their jobs, businessmen to hold their markets. But consumers, on the other hand, may want foreign competition to force down prices. Which goal shall have top priority? Clearly, how we evaluate a new tariff may be different depending on which set of goals we accept."

"Personal goals" are rationally set against "consumer wants," and everyone knows which side the cause of "citizenship" must favor. In fact, economists to a man are advocates of free trade. Yet a "rational" look at the situation, considering factors other than efficiency and maximum output, would clearly involve other questions. If in a free-trade situation comparative advantage leads the United States to produce goods from capital-intensive industries and import goods from labor-intensive industries, the nation might face unemployment problems even more horrific than those which seem likely under any circumstances in the late 1960s. The protectionists' argument that "it will be your turn next" is clearly selfish, but not necessarily wrong. This observer, in the cherished capacity of layman, strongly supports tariff reductions and removal, on the grounds that you cannot make omelets without breaking eggs, that these eggs are going to go rotten anyway, and that postponement and palliation will not lead to solutions of the unemployment problem. But the Task Force statement of the argument, identifying selfish goals on one side and consumer interest on the other, as though there were no "consumer interest" in the maintenance of jobs, is sufficiently incomplete to qualify as partisan.

Like students, economists resent the lack of "principle" in political decision. "Clear thinking on economic matters," the Task Force insists, "requires recognition of goals." In a functioning democracy, however, most people's goals are what operations researchers call minmax solutions. "Recognition" falsifies them by making some one aspect unduly prominent, which, in turn, makes economists' simplistic political solutions more plausible. "Economics for citizenship" has much in common with Engine Charlie Wilson's proposal that what was good for the country would be good for General Motors (which is what he really said, though it got publicized the other way around).

Anyway, as a practical matter, "citizenship" is a hopeless goal for instruction. Any stupidity can be defended as helping to promote it.

THE TASK FORCE—AND AFTER

Economic Education in the Schools, the Report of the National Task Force on Economic Education, was published in the fall of 1961. Five of its authors were economists, past or present officers of the American Economics Association; two (Moe Frankel of the Joint Council and Arno Bellack of Teachers College) were not.

Shortly before publication of the pamphlet, R. A. Gordon of the University of California, one of the task forcers, discussed the report in a talk before the Western Economic Association. "A superficial reader's first impression," he said, "may be that the Task Force has merely summarized what is in the standard sort of college textbook in elementary economics. I hope that a more careful reading will dispel this impression. We are careful to indicate what is essential and what can be safely omitted. We put up red flags to warn the teacher when the usual way of dealing with some involved topic is likely to confuse the student. We stress an elementary understanding of the broad and essential features of our kind of economy and of the important ways in which it differs from alternative ways of organizing economic life. . . ." In other words, the usual Principles of Economics course was cut down by the Task Force in hopes of making it suitable for high schools. But this course is almost universally regarded as poor ("A specter is haunting eco-

99

nomics;" wrote an AEA committee not long ago after an investigation of college instruction, "the specter of bad teaching"). To foist it on the high schools, via a nationwide early-morning television course, with all the authority of the AEA and the financial backing of CED and Ford, does not seem a profound contribution to education.

If anything is to be accomplished by university intervention in the affairs of the schools, professors must put into their work for younger students the same stretches of time and quality of thought they would devote to their graduate programs and their research. The notion that professors do the schools a favor when they deign to offer advice must be scotched from the beginning, and the men proposing school programs must be willing to subject themselves to criticism of the same severity (and praise of the same quality) they would expect from their colleagues when they publish original work. The Task Force backed away from the real problem in economic education by refusing to concern itself with "how the material should be presented in high schools," and must be condemned for accepting an assignment which in effect forbade consideration of the only area where a contribution could be made. But the report also suffers from numerous weaknesses of both thought and language. Seven of these feeble items are detailed in Appendix B; these seven do not exhaust the possible criticisms of the report.

The Task Force and the Joint Council have left open the question of what ought to be done in economics. The pamphlets and books recommended by the Materials Evaluation Committee are almost all abstract, dealing with general concepts and issues rather than with patterns of production and consumption of real goods and services. With a few exceptions—the *Petition of the Candlemakers*, Allen's *The Big Change*, Radford's *Prisoner of War Camp* —they are extremely light on names, dates, places, people, events. They seek to teach by telling. The Task Force itself is by no means happy with the materials list, and at this writing is seeking money to finance the preparation of new books and pamphlets.

Nobody knows how much economics could be taught through the use of intelligently prepared case studies, from which students (with the help of trained teachers) might induce economic generalizations. Though several members of the Task Force have privately expressed the belief that case studies would be valuable, the tenor of the report—and of the television series based on the report—harmonizes only with a traditionally taught Principles course. What little work has been done with the case approach— the Grinnell College experiment, the Reese pamphlet, some business-school oddities—was resolutely ignored.

Fortunately, the Task Force report has not discouraged the few economists who have been working, mostly with Joint Council groups, to improve economic education in the schools. By and large, they see little in the report that they can use, but they regard it as an important pat on the head from the arbiters of their professional future. "Whatever else the Task Force did," several of them have said, in identical words, "they made it respectable to take an interest in economic education." Only an extremely naïve observer could react to this testimonial with the shocked question, "Who needs *that?*"

COMPARATIVE SYSTEMS

The one widespread movement of genuine power in the social studies today is the drive toward the teaching of "comparative systems." Three states (Florida, Georgia, and Louisiana) have already passed laws requiring the high schools to teach a course in "Communism vs. Democracy" (Louisiana demands that every high-school student see the film "Communism on the Map" before receiving a diploma, a stipulation which at least one teacher has met by using the film as an example in the Propaganda unit of a Problems course). Most of what goes on under this label is, of course, highly

101

dishonest—an examination of half a dozen of the books and pamphlets actually used in schools to teach about Communism fails to turn up a single mention of the Communists' strongest argument, that the "surplus value" from a man's labor should be used for the good of the entire community, not for the profit of an employer. (Despite the eminence of the names associated with the book, and the avoidance of many of the usual name-calling puerilities, the Time, Inc.–Silver Burdette book *The Meaning of Communism* is not a great advance over its coarser rivals.) But even the *Masters of Deceit* approach is less ignorant than what usually appears in the newspapers and magazines; and, given the international situation, there is a limit to the objectivity about Russia and Communism which the community will tolerate in its schools. Serious people, as well as politicos and propagandists, are concerned about Americans' ignorance of institutions and attitudes other than their own, and in a fair number of schools the drive to "know your enemy" is joined to a more interesting attempt to break the student out of his ethnocentricity. An understanding of other people's governmental and economic systems, after all, is part of knowing the world in which you live.

But both teaching and learning about a different, complicated, literate culture present almost unimaginable difficulties. And, despite the attractive simplicity of their analyses, neither economics nor political science is a good tool for getting at the difficulties.

Economic and political "systems" do not exist *in vitro*. They are part of the human ecology, manifestations of cultures which include and to a large extent determine them. Economics as a discipline assumes at the root of its analyses pecuniary or consumption motives for human action; tradition is something that rational self-interest will knock down or get around, and magic is simply beyond the pale of thought. The study of economics is a product of emergent capitalism, and the utilitarian value system of the early nineteenth century is built into its foundation beyond possibility of removal.

Forty years have passed since Malinowski demonstrated, by his investigations of the Kula in the Trobriand Islands, that economic analysis is a culture-bound phenomenon. Similarly, political science rests on Graeco-Roman assumptions filtered first through the Renaissance and then by the religious wars of the sixteenth and seventeenth centuries. American and British political science—by far the most eminent branches of the subject—grew from further peculiarities in the rapidly shifting patterns of land tenure and land use that characterized long stretches of history in each nation. "We have not the notion," Matthew Arnold wrote nearly a century ago, "so familiar on the Continent and to antiquity, of *the State*—the nation in its collective and corporate character, entrusted with stringent power for the general advantage, and controlling individual wills in the name of an interest wider than that of individuals."

Within a given culture, economics and political science are viable disciplines. The search for relevance can be carried on in strict order, because the cultural framework of the "system" is bred in the student's bones and enshrined in his language. When the same definitions and categories are carried over to other cultures and other languages, however, they typically fail to make contact with reality. The disciplines themselves, in short, are highly ethnocentric.

People do not "choose to organize their economies in different ways." Existing societies are the inheritors of history; they rest less on rational self-interest than on culture patterns developed before and during history. Rapid changes of surface institutions, as the Roman and Ottoman and British empires learned, do not imply rapid changes in the realities of existence within the community. Changes in one's own culture, moreover, seem deceptively great. It is not a clean break with the past when a government that guaranteed the coinage, protected infant industries, recognized the limited liability corporation and subsidized canal and railroad building moves on to supervise banks, insure against unemployment,

103

recognize labor unions, and build dams. But it would be a monstrous wrench for the people of Ghana to drop tribal loyalties and duties to the extended family in favor of a consumption-motivated society. What proportion of American Indians have in fact become successfully functioning members of a Western European capitalist community?

Economic and political institutions are comprehensible only against the background of history. To understand the state farms of Russia, one must know something of the *oprichnina* (which also failed); to get at the realities of the collective farms, one must have some acquaintance with the *krestianskaia obshchina* which were "given" to the serfs at the time of the Emancipation. Words— especially words which are translations from another language— may be utterly deceptive. The Task Force writes: "Various democratic societies—the United Kingdom, the Scandinavian countries, and India, for example—have chosen to adopt socialism in varying degrees." But there is in reality no valid equation between the socialism of Sweden (a country that became rich late and sought to avoid the visible problems of countries that had grown rich too soon, a country that retains titles of nobility, that has ruled itself —and, at times, much of the rest of Europe—from the beginning of its history) and the socialism of India (a country based on communalism and caste, ruled by foreigners for half a millennium, poorer now than it was three or four hundred years ago). And the Christian socialism of Britain, planned by men who marched "to build a new Jerusalem on England's green and pleasant land," is something else again.

These obvious truths have been obscured by the similarities between Communist and capitalist economic theories (*viz.*, Oskar Lange), both of which rest on utilitarian (or "materialist") assumptions. In the Russian as in the American economy, first reliance is placed upon pecuniary motivation, which does not turn the trick in Africa or India or China (or, for that matter, much of Spain and southern Italy, and the *altiplano* of Boliva). To some extent, with incessant reservations and referrals to history, and careful avoidance of the vulgarities of GNP, the American and Russian economies can be compared; but "the economics of the underdeveloped nations" is not, so far, a viable discipline, because it unconsciously assumes specific and often unlikely alterations of the existing culture.

Further obscurities are introduced by the enormous impact of Western European nineteenth-century culture on the peoples of Asia and Africa—an impact wholly comparable to that of the sixteenth-century Spaniards on Middle America, or the Romans on Punic Carthage, or the Aryans on Mohenjo-daro. Their reaction is described by political scientists as well as by newspapers under the clearly inapplicable word "nationalism." To write, as the Task Force does, that "communism and capitalism are viewed today as active alternatives by most of the underdeveloped countries" is to play children's games. A country may, indeed, choose the horse it wishes to back in international races, but barring a soul-destroying break with its own past it must fit its economic "system" into an existing culture. American mental health might be greatly improved by a solid understanding of the fact that there are no remaining non-European cultures into which American-style capitalism (or, for that matter, Russian-style Communism) will conveniently fit. Rather than studying Japan as they now do, students might profitably look into the similarities and differences of European and Japanese "feudalism," for purposes of speculating on economic development.

You might as well fall flat on your face as lean over too far backward: a knowledge of economics is worth little, over the long run, without a knowledge of the inevitable limits of the discipline. As a subject for teaching, economics is in better case than most, because its boundary conditions are so clear, because it can accept so little from the other social sciences or from those aspects of reality which violate its assumptions. And the economist's habit

105

of mind is, I think (I have it myself), a useful corrective to folly in other fields, where the question of the alternative, the need for choice, is often ignored. Marshall's insight into the system-wide impact of change "at the margin" is a far better base for analysis than anything in the sociologist's lexicon of commentary about "opinion leadership." But if the economists are to function effectively in education, they will have to concentrate their work in those areas where the analysis is directly fruitful for understanding, and let the businessmen and the educators worry about "citizenship." And they will have to think hard about teaching.

IV

The Newer Behavioral Sciences:
Anthropology,
Psychology,
Sociology

Government and economics began as branches of philosophy, where metaphysics, epistemology, and ethics were given by other hands. When they broke off on their own, in the eighteenth and nineteenth centuries, it became apparent that many of the central concepts in the disciplines were descriptive rather than analytic. Economics assumes demand; political science assumes society: neither "marginal utility" nor the "indifference curve" tells anything about why people spend their substance for one economic good rather than another, and a term like "the State" (let alone "the nation") obviously covers a multitude of highly dissimilar patterns of behavior. Early economists and political scientists (the word "early" in this case extends at least to Veblen) made the mistake of resting their argument on the behavior of "unspoiled" or "savage" humans. Closer acquaintance with technologically primitive peoples led to the discovery that their behavior was very different from what had been assumed. Meanwhile, the sex-obsessed, death-bedeviled Europeans of the nineteenth century had been looking somewhat more closely at their *own* behavior. Many intellectuals began to feel that economics and political science assumed away what was most interesting in the study of man.

Ethnology (now "cultural anthropology"), psychology, and sociology are all attempts to get behind the cloak of rational explanation man wraps around his behavior. Because these disciplines proclaim similar goals, educational administrators are forever trying to put them together into a single block of study, usually under a name like "Social Relations." But as disciplines they do not fit together well; as George Homans puts it, "there is no general theory." Outlining a high-school course in Foundations of Human Behavior, the Brandeis sociologist Robert Feldmesser listed six examples of behavior which sets man off from other animals; anthropologists and psychologists would argue that at least three of these examples—"Using Language," "Learning," and "Living in Groups" —are to be found among other animals, too. Essential words like "family," "habit," even "language" and "group," have very different meanings in the three disciplines.

Both anthropology and psychology work from basing points in natural science. Bones, color, blood types, specialized features, susceptibility (or lack of it) to certain diseases give the anthropologist a very high class of evidence when he discusses the races of man; the physiology of the nervous system and the possibility of laboratory experiment are available to buttress claims of universality for some psychological theories. But the most important assertions of both these disciplines—and all the assertions of sociology—rest on highly partial evidence incompletely gathered and probably inadequately analyzed. The half-life of theories in all these fields has been exceedingly short. To devote one's life to any of these disciplines is to live on the edge of the volcano, which does not conduce to

110

confident teaching. "Psychology," says Ernest Hilgard of Stanford, "is in a strange stance. We're much happier about our methods than we are about the substantive knowledge. The highest agreement is on the more trivial aspects of the subject." Asked what the schools should do in their field, the most able and intelligent professors of the behavioral sciences almost invariably recommend stress on methods of investigation rather than on content.

To the extent that the word "method" in such a formulation means "habit of mind," the attempt to organize sense experience within the framework of the discipline, the goal is unassailable. When they recommend the teaching of their subjects, however, many behavioral scientists speak of "scientific method," something general to many fields and drawing its acceptability and prestige by faulty analogue to the physical sciences. (It is hard to understand, anyway, why students must work on the behavioral sciences to learn about "scientific method"; one would think the courses in science could do that job.) Weak content in a discipline cannot be seriously defended by the claim of good method—over the long run, method will be judged by the quality of content. In academic studies, too, the salt must have its savor or the work cannot be salted. The defensiveness of the best behavioral scientists is an inevitable reaction to the embarrassments they caused themselves and their colleagues by claiming too much in the heyday of social science theorizing. But nobody will blame an immature discipline for being near the beginning in the process of successive approximation that firms up the will to believe. The seminal ideas of literary and political thought, at this time, in this place, are those that lie behind the behavioral sciences. The words have become clichés—"culture," "class," "motivation"—but they enshrine data and notions that children will not find out about for themselves, and that must be taught. It is not only in the behavioral sciences that the teaching of the best we now know turns out later to have been the teaching of error.

Today the schools barely touch on the habits of mind of the

111

behavioral scientists. Some of the data come up, usually in horribly garbled form. What the behavioral sciences deal with is material that, inevitably, cuts near the bone; people at any age do not enjoy being told that their behavior is neither rational nor free. Teachers are usually ignorant, timid, or overenthusiastic in approaching the subjects. Partly because each of the disciplines has developed a highly specialized terminology (often unnecessarily specialized), little has been written which is both serious and readable on the school (or sometimes any other) level. Nearly all the interesting written material that does exist for school use is in the field of anthropology.

ANTHROPOLOGY

Herodotus and Marco Polo wrote ethnology; so did Francis Parkman; and so, in a sense, did Tocqueville. What sets modern anthropology apart is the attempt—ultimately hopeless, but rewarding in failure—to keep the observations separate from the prior learnings of the observer in his own home town. Anthropology seeks to relate the habits of a community to each other, in a systematic manner, and to relate these habit systems to the genetic characteristics of mankind. In the process, it has turned up a great quantity of data important to anyone who seeks to understand himself and his own society. But exactly *how* the data are important remains in most instances still to be discovered.

Anthropology's anchor to windward lies in the biological pattern common to all men, and in the social needs of a gregarious animal. People are born, mature, produce and consume, reproduce, age and die in all cultures; and because they live in groups they require some institutional framework for group decision making and for the control (if not suppression) of individual vices. They also need explanations of the confusing world around them—ideally, explanations that seem to give them power over their always menacing and ultimately fatal situation. And they need ways to handle their relations with outsiders, who worship different gods and practice a different (perhaps more potent) magic, who treat the great events of life with different ceremonies, whose societies make different demands on the individual member. History to the anthropologist is a catalogue, not of crimes and follies, but of cultural diffusions.

Gathering information about people's *Weltanschauung*, their rituals and social habits, their totems and taboos, must be highly rewarding work. Even though the goal be systematic, the effort itself retains the old-fashioned charm of contact with strange customs and beliefs; and the moment when the context becomes comprehensible, when the field observations lock together into a perception of system, must be one of the most joyous experiences of intellectual enterprise—made piquant because it must be enjoyed amongst people who do not have the vaguest notion of why the anthropologist is getting drunk. As a study, anthropology has forced the realization that something real and relevant to the human condition lies behind the strangest of foreign customs; and that the observer's own customs are a function of the history and situation of his own tribe, not necessarily a further advance in the march of progress. The study of anthropology launches a direct attack on ethnocentricity. Unfortunately, while pursuing this attack, anthropologists and teachers easily forget that however green other hills may be, they are *not* the hills of home.

It is difficult to get quality data in anthropology, and even more difficult to use the data carefully and well. Beliefs must be reconstructed from myths, institutions induced from an inevitably partial observation and participation. The danger of jumping to conclusions is omnipresent, magnified at all times by the difficulties of pulling thoughts out of a language not your own, by the human need to find explanations and the human tendency to cling to whatever explanations are first found. The obvious explanation for matrilineal societies is their failure to realize the male role in physio-

113

logical reproduction—which could be possible in societies which never domesticated animals. Most anthropologists now believe that the societies once thought to be the victims of this ignorance knew perfectly well where babies come from; they just weren't talking to visitors, even friendly visitors.

Anthropologists, moreover, have been most successful in dealing with preliterate and proto-literate societies, where the labor of the community is divided into coarse blocks rather than tiny subcells. Their bias, too, is toward systems in equilibrium, toward persistence, toward what David Riesman in another discipline has called "tradition-directed" societies. Change comes through adaptation to environment, through cultural diffusion, or through some mystery not far removed from magic. Literacy, by making possible the rapid diffusion of abstract ideas, institutionalizes change, especially trivial change, and blocks the anthropologist from the use of the tools by which he habitually distinguishes relevant from irrelevant data. What anthropologists can say with considerable authority, having done most of their work on rapidly disappearing or wholly vanished cultures, is that habits are interrelated, that any cultural change implies other changes within the system, and that such changes are always painful and often destructive, altering as they do the ecology of social existence.

Where these changes come from and what they mean in a technologically advanced and literate society is not the anthropologist's proper business; he does it badly, as Ruth Benedict, Geoffrey Gorer, Margaret Mead, and Ashley Montagu have so splendidly demonstrated. Reading a summary of one of the reports made at Endicott House, the anthropologist Douglas Oliver of Harvard grew angry at the phrase "when the Germans entered history"—but there is something to that phrase. Whether or not people without history are happy, they make better subjects for the anthropologists, because the relevant data are so much less extensive and so much more easily categorized. Just as economics and political science tend to be misleading when applied to "tradition-directed" communities, anthropology tends to be monumentally incomplete when applied to institutions (even long-standing institutions like the family) in technologically advanced and highly literate societies. Confronted with the varied patterning of income-based class stratification, the anthropologist observes naïvely; he sees the skull beneath the skin in a man of straw. (Thus an Oscar Lewis becomes a modern Mayhew—fascinating, intelligent, but leading nowhere.) Indeed, anthropology is often most impressive when it deals with the results of archaeology, where extraneous evidence is at an absolute minimum and the habit of mind reconstructs humanity from mud and stone and pottery and bones, and with archaic language, where the reference frames of words can be analyzed with a minimum of interference from current usage.

The material of anthropology is intrinsically attractive, and a fair amount of such material is in fact thrown at American students from an early age. Indians enter in third or fourth grade, geography is a litter of quaint customs, world history goes back to primitive man (very toothy, with receding forehead). Unfortunately, the Indians are on horseback, mostly, with big feathered bonnets, and the customs are almost always presented singly, and explained by environmental determinism. (Nearly all Americans believe that Eskimos spend most of their lives in snow-and-ice igloos.) "Individualized reading" often takes elementary-school children into anthropological subjects (and some of the pamphlets, particularly those of the childhood book clubs, are rather seriously meant, though Douglas Oliver, who has been reading them, finds them mostly erroneous in important respects). *Kon-Tiki* is probably the most popular single "outside-reading" book on the junior-high level.

Nothing at all systematic, however, seems to be attempted below the ninth-grade level. A handful of high schools—Verde Valley in Arizona, Edsel Ford in Dearborn, Germantown Friends in Philadelphia, the University of Chicago Laboratory School, the high

115

school in Columbus, Indiana—have tried out anthropology courses. Mrs. Malcolm Collier estimates that there are fifty such courses offered in American schools. Pennsylvania schools, now compelled to teach "World Cultures" by act of the state legislature, are looking rather wistfully to anthropology to bail them out. At Lexington, Massachusetts, one of the most startingly intelligent and successful of experimental social studies courses (designed mostly by Constance Murray of the high school) divides the ninth grade into four pieces, one for physical anthropology, one for archaeology, one for political science (the fall of the Greek and Roman Republics) and one for sociology (the role of the Church in medieval Europe).

What appears as anthropology in most World History courses, however, is fantastically ignorant. Thus, for example, the current edition of the Heath textbook (called *The Record of Mankind*, to add insult to injury) opens with the following:

> Man was first a savage, then a barbarian, and finally a civilized being. The *savage* depends almost entirely on nature. He secures food from wild plants and wild animals; he knows nothing of metals but makes his tools and weapons of stone, wood, and bone; he wears little or no clothing; and his home is merely a cave, a rock shelter, or a hut of bark. Such primitive folk still live in the interior of Africa and Australia. The *barbarian* has gained more control over nature than the savage. He plants seeds, has domesticated animals, and uses some metal implements. Most American Indians before the coming of Columbus and most of the Negroes in Africa may be classified as barbarians. . . .

Better materials in some quantity are available for high-school use. Gene Lisitzky's *Four Ways of Being Human*, written specifically for adolescents, is a straightforward, relatively serious look at the Semang, Eskimo, Maori, and Hopi cultures, by a writer who cares deeply about the subject and wants to see it taught at school. Kluckhohn's *Mirror for Man* seems to be within the capacities of

116

bright ninth graders (Lexington is using it), and Germantown Friends uses Margaret Mead's *Coming of Age in Samoa* with the same age group. Anne Terry White's *Lost Worlds* is accurate romance. A few schools have successfully used George Spindler's Stanford series of case studies. A number of paperbacks deal with physical anthropology in a popular yet essentially correct manner. Adequate films, however, are scarce. Louis Larson of Georgia State, who came into contact with schoolchildren while digging up the remains of the largest known Cherokee settlement and placing a museum on the site, says that he has found four—*The Hunters, The Moon's Necklace, Lascaux,* and *Nanook of the North*—which he would be willing to show to students. (*Lascaux* is of course an art film; Larson finds it invaluable in teaching his college students about sympathetic magic.) Nobody in the field seems to believe that there are more than eight or ten films on anthropology that are worth more than the match it would take to burn them—and most of these, Douglas Oliver says, are Canadian.

Considering the interest of the subject, its presence in pieces in the existing curriculum, and the current intellectual vitality of the discipline, the introduction of more serious instruction in anthropology seems a practical proposition. Early in 1962, the American Anthropological Association established an Anthropology Curriculum Study Project under the direction of Mrs. Malcolm Collier. That summer, the project worked on first drafts of an anthropologist's view of "The Emergence of Civilizations" (by Jack Ellison, for high-school World History), a case study of the Kiowa (by Alice Marriott), and a three-unit course in New York State history, presenting the Iroquois, "the Homespun Age" on upstate farms, and the City as three separate cultures (by Hazel Hertzberg of Suffern Junior High School). Robert Hanvey of the University of Chicago Lab School also worked during the summer for the project, developing what Mrs. Collier describes as "a rationale and description of several units presenting traditional historical materials within anthropological concepts." Meanwhile, Douglas Oliver has put together a small group of outstanding university anthropologists to develop materials (both films and pamphlets) for anthropology units throughout the school years—from first grade through graduate school. What is impressive about both these ventures is the imagination that has gone into the search for teaching ideas, the interest in finding specific pieces of work rather than identifying "concepts" to be taught. Oliver, for example, is considering a study of the frontier—the border between cultivators and hunters—as a theme that runs through history. He has Howard Mumford Jones and some Jungian psychologists working (separately) on the teaching of myths; and he has the magnificent Sherwood Washburn of Minnesota relating animal and human behavior —for example, in crowded habitats—for the edification of children. Mrs. Collier wants to offer the schools, among other tidbits, an anthropological study of the slave society in the South in the years just prior to the Civil War.

But the teaching of anthropology is going to be tricky. Comparison is the essence of the subject, and the carrying over of values from one's own culture to another typically hinders understanding and appears illegitimate. Most teachers and students who attempt elementary anthropology trip rapidly into the land of cultural relativism, which is a form of moral laziness (nobody really need feel ashamed of himself for disapproving of cannibalism) and which causes the material to burn with brief excitement and then seem meaningless.

The "curriculum guides" for existing anthropology courses in the schools are almost uniformly distressing. One and all, they place emphasis on the argument that men are much more alike than they are different, which is simply an isolated fact and a rather dull one (though Ernestine Friedl of Brooklyn College has thought of an economical way to teach it, by comparing a film of a gorilla band with *The Hunters,* to show the enormous gap in social organization between the apes and the most "primitive" men). Then they stress the enormous adaptability of man, which is either a truism (man has survived to live in all sorts of unwholesome places, as have sharks, insects, microbes, and viruses) or a falsism (applying as it does to a species rather than to individuals or particular cultures). None of these guides, incidentally, carries on from the idea of adaptability to the logical corollary that different races ought to intermarry like mad, to increase the genetic possibilities of adaptation. Evolution, a central idea in physical anthropology and a difficult one in cultural anthropology, is equated with progress, ignoring the case Lewis Mumford argues for the proposition that natural selection among men has operated on the principle that nice guys finish last, making man the urbanized son of a bitch he is today.

The schools, finally, with their emphasis on citizenship, are only too willing to accept the imperial pretensions of any academic discipline, and eagerly welcome the anthropologists who want to deal with what Bernard DeVoto once called "the American Islanders." Phrases like "the culture of the slums" and "the culture of factories," employed allegedly as anthropological terms, were already to the fore in the discussion of anthropology as a school subject at the November, 1961, meeting of the National Council for the Social Studies. Anthropology is essential for a study of the African, but not easily applicable to "the Negro Problem." Potlatch parties are not legitimately related, except through a trivial common ancestry in boasting, to "conspicuous consumption," which is a function of social mobility. Self-control as well as energy and intelligence will be demanded from the anthropologists who take an interest in the schools.

PSYCHOLOGY

Among the few characteristics that can definitely be ascribed to the scientific habit of mind (or "scientific method") is the belief that profundity will produce simplicity. Walter Michels of Bryn

119

Mawr a few years ago told a meeting of the Educational Testing Service that physics was really a very simple subject—"anything complicated, we call chemistry." As all the natural world reduces ultimately, though not necessarily usefully, to the sought-for simplicities of physics, all of human behavior reduces to the hoped-for simplicities of psychology. For the anthropologist, it is enough to say that certain behavior is learned, and that this learning process is accompanied in this culture by certain rituals. The psychologist wants to know what is meant by, what process lies behind, a word like "learning." Anthropology seeks merely to identify normal and aberrant behavior; psychology looks for the roots of aberration and the causes of the norms.

Psychology is a very ancient study, going back at least to the Sophists. Until near the turn of this century, however, it was mostly conducted either by philosophers on a basis of *a priori* reasoning (or its first cousin, introspection), or by medical doctors (often enough quacks) on a basis of undigested experience with patients. Those sections of psychology which deal with aberration ("clinical psychology," in current terminology) have been made far more difficult by the so-far unpredictable oddities of occurrence and remission in mental disease. ("The first question adolescents will ask me," says Ernest Hilgard, "is, 'Does psychotherapy work?' And what answer can I give them?") Modern psychology had a German mother, but its father was probably William James, himself both a professional philosopher and a medical doctor, whose insistence on *a posteriori* reasoning led him to pragmatism and to an intelligently skeptical support for psychological experimentation.

Ultimately, all psychology must have a physiological base: "thought" itself is a physiological phenomenon, grossly measurable through the electroencephalogram, and visible in certain situations through involuntary physical reactions in heartbeat, skin temperature, the operation of sweat glands, etc. The locus of operating stimulus in the central nervous system can often be identified; in-

120

deed, psychologist-physiologists have been able to stimulate desired reactions by both animals and men through both electrical and chemical alterations of the environment of specific cell assemblies in the brain. In recent years, rather quietly, emphasis in both clinical and experimental psychology has shifted toward biological rather than strictly behavioral research, toward the treatment of mental illness by drugs and the analysis of phenomena like perception through physical measurements. There is also an expanding school of cyberneticists, who attempt to duplicate through electronic gadgetry some of the more puzzling aspects of human psychology, in the hopes of proving out psychological theories through analogy with purely electronic behavior.

Behavioral psychology itself has grown considerably in sophistication, dropping the earlier easy equation between animal and human behavior and developing more detailed statistical techniques to compensate for the inevitably small samples involved in the study. (Behavioral scientists who complain that the public at large distrusts "statistical knowledge" can argue with reason that all knowledge is statistical; but there remains a great difference between the statistics of the physicist, which start with samples of 10^7 and work up, and the statistics of the social scientists, which rarely reach a sampling base of 10^4. Randomization leaves the individual still at the mercy of the rub of the green, and from this vantage point the stability of the norm seems unimportant.) Psychological testing, which is directly salable, remains a foundation of the prestige of the field, though there do not seem to be very many very good tests or intelligent testers. One of the really delightful little facts in academic life is that graduate students in psychology always win the top average score on intelligence tests designed (scientifically, of course) by people who were recently graduate students in psychology. Clever (or "projective") tests are pregnant with interesting ideas in the hands of clever (or "projective") analysts of the results; and the advertising industry has become a large-scale

121

consumer of such services. Like the other behavioral sciences, psychology suffers, sometimes grievously, from a failure to appreciate the difference between the definition of terms and the construction of theories. To say that a need for "drive reduction" causes activities that reduce the drive is to dribble from the mouth.

Though psychoanalysts, starting with Freud, have written extensively about historical figures, psychologists are usually the most unhistorical of the social or behavioral scientists. Much of the evidence they require tends to perish with the subject, and psychological generalizations from written records (invariably self-serving, but in greatly varying ways) must have dubious validity. Oddly enough, however, the teaching of elementary psychology tends to operate within a historical frame. While the historians themselves disregard their greatest leaders in the rush for current interpretation, the psychologists plod their students through Ebbinghaus and Pavlov and Thorndike, with full knowledge that the sands on which these theories rested have shifted out of respectable sight. At the same time, anything predating Wundt and James and Freud is taboo, and psychology students rarely know that the controversies between the behaviorists and the Gestalt psychologists are quite closely related to the differences over epistemology between Aristotle and Plato, or that the idea of "consciousness" contains a residue of debt to Descartes. A visitor who has looked at French as well as American teaching of psychology cannot resist the feeling that French students gain something from coming to the subject at the end of an intensive year of philosophy. Both were doubtless wrong, but Bergson was a much more interesting thinker—and a much better source for testable hypotheses—than Watson.

Still, we must live with what we have, and part of the academic scene is the intellectual parochialism of the psychology department (though not necessarily of individual psychologists). Most people who have thought about the matter believe that it is better to know something of the roots of one's reactions to experience than to stagger about in a miasma of guilt or a certainty of rectitude based on unconscious selectivity of perception. The amateur psychologist is rapidly assuming the role once played in American life by the fo'c'sle lawyer; and schoolchildren themselves can scarcely avoid contact with words like "IQ," "motivation," "personality," "guidance," even "displacement" and the like. A fair amount of "psychology" (even if it is only opinions about "human nature") is going to be picked up by virtually every student. "This, too," as David McClelland of Harvard puts it, somewhat sourly, "is part of our civilization." And there would doubtless be some value in giving adolescents a feeling for the disciplined investigation of such notions.

At present, most psychology teaching in the schools is done by teachers acting *in loco parentis* on questions of sex, ethics, and family relations. Few teachers have studied the subject beyond the introductory level, and the educational psychology course in teacher-training institutions is almost always a confused gabble of contradictory theories of learning, intelligence, and memory, definitions of words like "withdrawal," "frustration," and "aggression," an introduction to elementary statistics, and hortatory statements of the importance of being nice to children. In some training courses, highly technical tools of somewhat dubious value, such as "psychodrama," are also recommended, as one might recommend a recipe for a *coq au vin*.

Occasional courses in psychology are taught on the high-school level. Even a fairly large sample of schools would not turn up enough such courses to justify making statements about them, but they seem to be awful. The textbooks are dogmatic, oriented toward "life adjustment" and similar uses, and often plainly distressing. Thus, *Psychology for Living* by Herbert Sorensen and Marguerite Malms, discovered in actual use in a Midwestern high school, states that "The ability to get along with people is called social intelli-

123

gence. . . . This is an intelligence which is different in many ways from abstract or idea intelligence. Nevertheless, there is, of course, a relationship between them. Usually people who have good minds, as we say of people who rank well in abstract intelligence, get along better with people than do those of poorer minds. The general evidence for that is found in the fact that people in positions of leadership usually have high intelligence." Note the "scientific method," the evidence for the generalization.

Experimental psychologists who have looked into the school situation feel that what is now done in this area should be scrapped almost entirely. Those who believe psychology should be formally taught (most psychologists seem to feel the high schools should stay away from the subject) would like to see it regarded as a laboratory science, with students as far as possible performing their own experiments. "Students can be the subjects," says Neal Miller of Yale. "You could use a motion-picture camera as a device for presenting situations. You could present optical illusions—what causes this? Are eye movements involved? Is that the only thing? Could you check it?—Yes, Archimedes' spiral. Check one eye to the other; it must be something in the brain. There are lots of experiments in the area of perception. You could use Hadley Cantril's film on illusions. Find out whether people go to left or right in symmetrical situations. Repeat Thorndike's experiment of drawing a line of specified length while blindfolded. For some phases, you might even get a magician in—they're very good at controlling behavior." Others can see no reasons why Skinner's pigeons cannot be trained by high-school as well as college students. Experimental psychologists generally would concentrate on the area where a technique is known to work without too much curvefitting. Hilgard would like to teach the use of investigations of identical and fraternal twins as evidence in the nature-nurture controversy (is intelligence determined by heredity or environment?), to demonstrate that psychological questions can be studied with elegance and

124

precision (a far more significant notion than the usual bland statement about "studying human behavior objectively"). Everyone would want much more emphasis than is now given to physiology. Robert Sears of Stanford, whose wife is a child psychologist, feels that some of this work could be successfully brought down to the later years of the elementary school, "when students have learned that there is such a thing as a large body of systematic knowledge." Sears was impressed by the quality of the questions he was asked after he made a presentation on the central nervous system to an elementary-school assembly.

Ronald Lippitt of Michigan reports interesting results from a more elaborate introduction of psychology in elementary schools. Operating on the hypothesis that the power structure and affectional structure of the elementary classroom might contain factors antagonistic to learning, Lippitt and a group of teachers sent sixth graders in teams of three to investigate what was happening in second-grade classrooms in the same school, organize their observations, and report back to home room. Whether such activity by "little researchers" can provide similar clarifications in the absence of big researchers remains, of course, to be proved; but the idea is both delightful and plausible.

High-school teachers who are working toward psychology courses tend to concentrate on "social psychology," attempting to bring data, method, and theory to bear on students' own problems. The "motivation" here is obvious—but so is the student's chance (and "motivation") to cheat the teacher; many can play at these games. This observer feels a good deal of reluctance about an emphasis on social psychology, partly because exclusive interest in the self and its aches is a prime symptom of Oblomovitis, partly because of the dreadful humorlessness that afflicts the social sciences at large, but the social psychologists in particular, when dealing with adolescents. But there are many intelligent teachers who believe passionately in this approach and who can get students talking,

125

reading, and thinking to some purpose—and it is always possible that what one teacher can do others can be trained to do.

From the classroom:

At the Lincoln-Sudbury High School about thirty miles from Boston, Paul Mitchell, chairman of the social studies department, is trying to get some abstract ideas into the heads of an average eleventh-grade American History class. Mitchell is a lean, tense bachelor in his forties, with a clipped speech and vast reserves of nervous energy. A product of St. Michael's College in Vermont, with graduate work at Clark Institute, he is a man who takes learning seriously and demands it from his students. He teaches a remarkably ambitious course in Russian History, built in part on his own library (kept at the school, the largest such collection in an American high school, available to students), in part on his observations during a summer's travel in the Soviet Union, camping out in a Volkswagen to the amazement of the people's police. His teaching pattern alternates great pressure from the front of the room with unstructured discussion, and he is forever working on the students' own situation to pull them into what he is doing. Over the blackboard runs a big banner: "And This Too Shall Pass Away." The topic of this class—Mitchell has virtually abandoned chronology as a structure for history—is the reason for the growth of pragmatism in the United States.

"Pragmatism is difficult," Mitchell says "one, because you're not interested; two, because it's philosophy, and you don't know any philosophy. But I told you I was optimistic.

"Now, pragmatism sees a world in motion. You don't match something against the transcendentalists' standard of truth. You do it, see if it brings you nearer your goal; if it does, it's good. . . .

"Now, this nebulous thing democracy that six weeks ago you couldn't define, you thought it was justice and virtue. People living

126

in the democracy welcomed a philosophy that told them the meaning of all these things was being developed in their society. You welcome it, too.

"All right. I ask you, 'What's society?' "

There is no answer, but the class stirs a little nervously. Mitchell speaks to the girls: "You don't feel like getting dressed. You come down to breakfast in blue jeans, ready to go to school. What does your mother say?"

A girl says, " 'Go upstairs and change your clothes.' "

"And you do it."

"Yes."

"Why?"

The girl shrugs her shoulders.

"How many of you dislike school? How many of you would rather be doing something else?"

About two-thirds of the class raise hands. "Then why are you here? Why don't you walk out the door?"

"Why don't *you* walk out the door?" a boy tries.

"I like school," Mitchell says. "I enjoy teaching."

Reasons come up from the floor—you've got to have a high-school diploma, going to college, parents insist. "Okay," Mitchell says. "I accuse you of being hypocrites." No defense is offered. "What's a society?" Mitchell says again, ruminatively. "Would you say this classroom is a society?"

A boy says, "Yes."

"Why?"

"We're all doing the same thing. I mean, we're all in the same room, supposedly listening to you."

"You're *listening?*" Mitchell says incredulously. "I'm a human being, you're a human being, there is no difference between us, you tremble . . . No, you're right. The classroom is a society.

"Pragmatism says, 'Values are made by the society.' You lived through it, from the moment you were born. You said, 'Mama.'

127

Then you said, 'Good morning, Grandma.' You did what you were expected to do. You go to church, you come here to school, to my classroom.

"Pragmatism says, 'Truth is what works.' People on the go like the concept that rightness and wrongness is determined by what works, in their society. How happy for them, and for you . . .

"The world is divided into Believers and Thinkers. I want you to be Thinkers, not Believers. If you just write all this down on an exam, give me back what I've been saying instead of finding your own examples, welcome to the Believers. I'll be sad, because it will mean I failed; and, what's more to the point, you'll be sad, because it will mean *you* failed. . . . I'll see you tomorrow, because you have no choice."

At Watchung Hills Regional High School, near Plainfield, New Jersey, about thirty miles from New York on overcrowded roads, Warner Fletcher, retiring chairman of the social studies department, is sweating a seminar group of nine twelfth graders, none of them in the college-preparatory track, through a course in Human Relations. He is a stocky, avuncular bachelor with a bushy, Germanic mustache; and he works hard and patiently. He has these slightly-below-average students reading Edgar Friedenberg's *The Vanishing Adolescent,* a book of considerably greater sophistication and difficulty than any of the textbooks for a Problems of Democracy course; and, with two exceptions, the class is actually reading it, and taking something from it. This day's discussion is considerably enlivened by the fact that one of the students in the school was killed the night before in an automobile accident.

"What has changed?" Fletcher asks. "It *is* different. Life for you is not what life was for me when I was your age. When I was in high school, nobody had a car. Let's go back to the theory— 'biological developments establishing needs which are met by significant adults in a particular community at a specific time.' . . .

128

"I hope we got over that argument that God just decided that that sixteen-year-old kid was going to die last night. What *is* happening in the world when young adolescents are killing themselves in hot rods? What is happening when kids eighteen years old have no idea of where they're going? 'The significant adults'—what have they done? Okay, Rosalyn."

A girl says, "When *they* were eighteen years old, they never found themselves. So now they're forcing their kids to go to college."

The next girl tries, "They were always like that, but maybe not in the same way—they didn't have hot rods, maybe they wanted them. They feel guilty for what they didn't do."

Yet another girl says, "We expect too much of teen-agers. They make greater demands on us, ask teen-agers to take greater responsibility."

"Remember," Fletcher says, "we're talking three factors, comparing them against twenty years ago—needs, significant adults, particular community."

One of the girls says, "We have all these different means of entertainment. Oh, everything is different, we have to live with the things we have."

Fletcher says, "I think you have much greater purchasing power, and that's important."

A girl says, "It's easier for us to run away from things."

"You are," Fletcher comments, "enormously freer to want . . ." Later: "You never had a date, when I was your age, before you were sixteen or seventeen years old. Nobody's saying anything's wrong, just that significant adults think it's wrong . . ."

Eventually, Fletcher pulls out the summary he wants:

"One, you have more purchasing power.

"Two, the dating age—the impact of sex has become enormously greater.

"Three, the practical difficulty of making a life choice is greater. Jobs require much more specialized training. . . ."

129

Watchung Hills, now returned to a more traditional curriculum, must have been one of the most interesting experiments in American education. What tore down much of the experimental structure was an unlucky controversy over the teaching of *The Catcher in the Rye,* and an attempt not only at real student government but at a critique of town government by students after a month of serious, on-the-spot investigation of how different municipal functions were handled. The result of this meddling by juveniles was, inevitably, a complaint that the new program was too expensive to be borne by the taxpayers.

Fletcher's "terminal program" seniors handled the material he gave them about as well as adolescents do; they had undoubtedly gained something from Fletcher's and Gordon Neisser's social-psychology (in many places psychoanalytic) view of human institutions and events, throughout history and into the present. Better students had also gained something from an ambitious reading list, including (for World History) excerpts from Benedict, Homans, Tacitus, Bowra, Muller, Herodotus, H. G. Wells, Adam Smith, Freud, Machiavelli, Locke, Rousseau, Dewey, and Linton —plus documents. Yet bright seniors in a Problems class, taking up American foreign policy and technical assistance, seemed to retain in their discussion groups the typical uninformed good-will attitudes of adolescents elsewhere who had never passed through the fire of thought. "They are," Neisser said, "terribly ignorant."

Given an erg or so of push by a visitor, however, Neisser's discussion groups began talking about their ignorance and wondering how to remedy it. To be conscious of and queasy about one's own ignorance is, of course, the visible mark of a good education. For all the romantic mish-mash of the need to have faith in science which characterized what Fletcher and Neisser wrote about their program, they seem to have known what they were doing in classrooms. We do not have so many such teachers that we can afford to waste them.

130

SOCIOLOGY

There is no borderline between social psychology and sociology, just as there is no border between the sociology and anthropology of a primitive village. Indeed, there are very few borderlines, very few informing postulates, around sociology as a study; there seems to be no discipline, no habit of mind, no device for the exclusion of irrelevance. The great bulk of what passes for sociology, not only before the public but within the field, is a tedious redefinition or quantification of common-sense notions. As Ernest van den Haag once said about yet another report proving that people tend to marry people from the same or contiguous social-class groups, religious groups, geographical groups, education groups, national-origins groups, and so forth, "It may be sociology, but it isn't news."

What is perhaps the central notion in sociology is best expressed by the Freudian assertion that "there are no accidents." All parts of the social system are interrelated—not only institutions, as in anthropology, but attitudes as well. Latent and manifest, the parts contribute to each other's functioning and change, somehow, *pari passu.* Dealing with far more complex societies than the anthropologist usually tackles, the sociologist relies on his perception of patterns in accumulations of both factual and projective data. Such data have become available in uncontrollable quantities during the last twenty years, leaving the sociologists euphoric about their opportunities and terribly confused about what they know and don't know. There are correlations all over the place, but not many of them stand up as causes. Gone are the days when a Marx could find the source of a man's thought in his societal role, when a Weber could emphasize secret societies, when a Tawney could equate Protestantism with the rise of capitalism, when a Lynd in Middletown or a Warner in Yankee City could stalk about putting

131

convenient labels on everything in sight. The Marxists were first with the attitude and first with the disillusionment—before the turn of the century they had to posit a *Lumpenproletariat,* too broken to protest, too dumb to care, too venal to cooperate.

During the last thirty years, sociology has made its contributions in those areas where restrictions in the focus of the study have provided boundary conditions for the data to be considered. Studying the factory, the university, the isolated group (labor union, bar association, juvenile gang, medical association, criminals in jail, etc.), the imaginative sociologist may be able to encompass in his collection of variables all the elements that influence the observed phenomenon. Even here, the investigator has to be awfully good. The ways in which data are collected always influence the data received, in the natural as well as the social sciences; but as anyone knows who has ever examined any number of sociological questionnaires, the sociologist can actually determine the data he will receive by his approach to his study. Somewhere, in the narrow range between the featureless visage of random accumulation and the waxed mustache of predetermined results, there is an intelligent human face to sociology; but it comes to view only occasionally.

There is also, of course, a classic sociology, which grows out of attempts to explain history. From this sociology come the abstract structures with which the field made its reputation—the notions of societal role and social class, family function, group formation, attitude development, and the like. The followers of this tradition seek general theories rather than pin-point data; among the more important representatives are Talcott Parsons, George Homans, and Marion Levy. Such sociologists, unfortunately, are usually not much interested in teaching on the lower levels (though Homans has been persuaded to work on revisions of a history course). Conscious of the overwhelming intellectual disarray of their discipline, they see little they can teach that they would wish children to know.

Within sociology itself, what might be called the humanist tradition of Homans and company is slowly returning to the center of the stage, and the "scientists" are retreating below stairs, where they will be, most of them, much more comfortable. They have been and still are an embarrassment to the social sciences as a community, because they have been so consistently simple-minded and wrong in their diagnoses of and prescriptions for the societies they have studied. Unfortunately, it is this group which finds new status for itself in the attempt to promote sociology for the schools (largely on the rather amusing grounds that the field today fails to recruit good students). Recently, the chairman of the committee which is trying to get National Science Foundation money to create sociology courses had occasion to list what he considered "the basic concepts of my discipline." They ran as follows:

1. The behavior of individuals is in part a function of group forces on them.

2. Some of the strains and tensions in individuals are a function of conflicts in culture and social structure.

3. One's location in the social structure influences one's perception of the world.

4. Conformity is a function of the norms of the group, and different groups have different norms.

5. Elements of the social structure have latent as well as manifest functions.

6. Events have multiple causations.

7. You can study human behavior through the scientific method.

Except for the last item, which doesn't mean anything unless "scientific method" is defined, the list would have drawn the strongest sort of agreement ("I've always said so m'self") from Jonathan Swift. In the seventh decade of the twentieth century, it fits neatly into the pigeonhole labeled Ho-Hum. All these "concepts" are part of the pervasive common sense of the middlebrow American culture, and most of them will become part of the

133

equipment of most reasonably intelligent people, whether or not they study sociology.

Worst of all, the "scientific" sociologists are antihistorical. One of the more interesting approaches to giving children some notion of social structure is the experimental ninth-grade course in Lexington, which takes the last quarter of the year for a study of the role of the Church in medieval Europe. Most sociologists who have been told about it have reacted negatively, simply because the subject is not contemporary and cannot be approached through sociological data-gathering techniques. Asked what they would like children to study, they usually suggest activities like those proposed by one of their in-group at a recent conference—a survey of the breakfast foods consumed by other students and a questionnaire about who the heroes are at school. Such suggestions grievously underestimate the risibility—and the pre-existing information—of adolescents. Men who emphasize "peer groups" and "norms" so strongly as the sociologists do should feel greater respect for the quality of the grapevine (and for the tenacity that keeps secrets out of the grapevine) in an adolescent community. The do-your-own-study approach also neglects the intense difficulty of securing valid data with sociological tools; and the answer made to this objection—that students will learn about the difficulty, which is educational, too—cannot be taken seriously.

Academic sociologists of any persuasion would doubtless do better than the textbook authors and publishers who now peddle sociology to the schools in the form of guidance materials and life-adjustment courses. And there is an argument to be made for the proposition that isolated sections of sociology—particularly those relating to occupations, and to the influence of social structure on adolescent behavior—might be, if rigorous in their admission of data and elegant in their presentation, both useful and educational in the secondary schools. The "study of society by the scien-

134

tific method," however (resting as it usually does on faulty extrapolations of erroneous perceptions of data gathered without criteria of significance), is no more defensible than current events as a school subject.

V

*Puzzles, Problems,
and Difficulties*

The two-legged ape became *Homo sapiens* at the instant of conscious recognition that there was something he could do to change the world around him. (In mythology, this is the moment when man steals fire from the gods.) We measure intelligence, among children and animals, as the ability to analyze tasks and then perform them. People in "advanced" cultures consider themselves superior to people in "primitive" cultures, and adults consider themselves superior to children, because they feel better equipped to discover what is malleable in reality and then to hammer effectively upon it. Within any culture, education is seen as the initiation into effective ways (which may be magical) of perceiving and handling reality, of "solving problems."

In the nineteenth century, most educators believed that there was a general problem-solving capacity in the individual, which could be strengthened for use by exercises, the way a boxer's punch is strengthened by roadwork. The "mental discipline" acquired in the study of Latin, or by the memorization of historical data, would strengthen the problem-solving muscles. Then, at the end of the century, experiments by budding psychologists demonstrated that scholastic exercise did not necessarily improve problem-solving performance. The mind was not a muscle, there was no "mental discipline."

The earlier belief has never wholly died out. Math teachers (and Task Force economists) like to argue that training in their subject leads people to "think logically." A recent theory, from Hebb and Rice, proposes that slum children inadequately stimulated in early childhood are handicapped for life—which is, of course, merely a variant of the "exercise" approach. Nevertheless, as an argument in sophisticated circles, "mental discipline" is thoroughly discredited.

In the heyday of behaviorism, which followed upon the demise of "mental discipline," educators insisted on immediate utility or enjoyment as the only reason for teaching anything. Thorndike wrote that all learning came by the formation of stimulus-response bonds, which became habits. ("When a child writes sixteen as 61 or finds 428 as the sum of $15+19+16+18$ or gives 642 as an answer to 27×36, or says that 4 divided by ¼ = 1, we are tempted to consider him mentally perverse, forgetting or perhaps never having considered that he goes wrong for exactly the same general reason that we go right, namely, the general law of habit formation.") The curriculum, even as seen by the Progressives who most disliked Thorndike, was to be an organization of those bonds that would make the most useful habits in later life.

This demand for instant utility, which survives in many educational theorists and administrators as a kind of vestigial tail, produced a number of embarrassments, the worst of them being its denial of the possibility of preparing children for change in a world that was changing with fearful rapidity. There was, fortunately, an escape available within the theory. Even the primitive experiments of Thorndike and Woodworth in 1901 had left room for the belief that some improvements in problem solving were possible through training, provided there was close analogy between the previous scholastic task and the new problem to be solved. The range of permissible analogies expanded rapidly, and presently the Progressives were asserting that problem-solving capacity could be developed *directly* by building schoolwork around problems and generalizing the solution techniques. Though most of Progressivism is (perhaps unfortunately) dead, this argument continues as a central article of faith in American education. It is only now beginning to yield to Jerome Bruner's gentle pushing on behalf of "cognitive activity," which obviously includes the organization of perceptions as well as the performance of tasks.

"Problem solving" is superficially a most attractive approach to the difficulties of education. It seems to imply induction as a method, and it "brings reality to the classroom" instead of rummaging around among bags of bones for scholastic examples. In social studies, "historical problems" give the color of adversary proceedings to what happened in the past, while "current problems" lead the student to participation in adult conversations and activities. Backed by the political influence of the utilitarians and the prestige of the psychologists, "problem solving" is today the official method of the social studies program.

In elementary school, the words don't mean much. "To develop a general concept of the United States," says Boston's Curriculum Guide for Geography in Grade IV, "use the problem approach, e.g., in the song 'America the Beautiful' what is meant by the phrase 'from sea to shining sea'?" It is probably possible (though quite difficult) to structure elementary-school social studies material so that it presents puzzles to solve—Larry Senesh is doing something of the sort in Elkhart. But the typical "widening circles"

141

strategy—moving the child through six or eight or (most recently, in California) fourteen steps from his home through his neighborhood, city, state, country, continent, hemisphere, political alliance, globe—requires the emptying of so large a grab bag of miscellaneous information that the child never has time to solve anything. "Projects," in which committees of children report on weaving in the colonies, or build medieval villages, or stage a skit entitled "This Is Your Life, Mahatma Gandhi!" do not of course involve the kind of problem solving the psychologists mean, though like all human activity they present "problems" to be solved.

Two courses in the junior-high program are pregnant with possibilities for problem solving—the group guidance "world of work" hour offered in the home room or by the social studies teacher, and the Civics course. In many schools, vocational orientation leads to a very real problem solving by students, who must decide at some time in eighth grade whether they wish to try a college-preparatory, "business," or skilled-trade curriculum in the high school. Personal problems are often touched on in these courses, quite gingerly, because the child is supposed to learn "who he is" (as philosophers have said for millennia, the one impossible task) before leaving junior high school. Civics courses, more often than not, will be built around local problems (ranging from legislative reapportionment to the need for new fire engines, depending on local situations) and how the community decided to handle them.

The *locus classicus* of the problems approach is, of course, the Problems of American Democracy class in the high school. (Few people seem to remember that this course was originally designed, by Harold Rugg, for the junior highs—and that Rugg's junior-high textbooks, for all their simple-minded liberalism, are still the most interesting and vital material ever prepared specifically for such a program.) Here the major issues that are agitating the newspapers are trotted out for class discussion, and students go off

142

to read up on the problem and report back. In some schools, students themselves choose the problem on which they wish to work. The bias here is completely contemporary—no discussion of the school segregation "problem" ever goes back to education in the Southern states in the years before the First World War, and there is rarely anything from the period preceding Brown v. Topeka Board of Education, 1954—and the sources are almost always newspaper and magazine articles, plus encyclopedias, and, very occasionally, a current book. Several reports from "PAD" classrooms have already appeared in this book; they are all dreadful. In five years of visiting American schools, I have never seen a Problems of Democracy class of any distinction whatever.

"Problem solving" as a general approach invariably and inevitably fails to produce a viable education in the social studies. The method is not inductive, because the problems are chosen for their "reality" rather than for their importance to disciplined perception, which means there is nothing to induce. In history, the Bank gets all tied up with the personalities of Hamilton and Jackson, and trust busting wears a walrus mustache; in "current problems," current political attitudes and the puerilities of the newspaper columnists dominate the work. "Reality" is always perceived in common-sense terms, which are intrinsically misleading—there is, for example, no excuse for a school discussion which uses words like "liberal" and "conservative" as though they had a known meaning. "The problems approach is, I think, a pernicious one," says Frank Freidel of Harvard, who has worked with teachers in a number of summer institutes, and cares enough about high-school history to serve as a vice-president of the New England Council for the Social Studies. "It leads students to wrong conclusions."

But there is something more fundamentally wrong with the problems approach, and with "problem solving" as a goal. The word "problem" is too general, and its use conceals essential divi-

143

sions among different kinds of tasks. The British philosopher T. D. Weldon, in his book *The Vocabulary of Politics,* makes the necessary distinction between "puzzles, problems and difficulties."

"A puzzle," Weldon writes, "is deliberately made up. . . . There is . . . a certifiably correct way of solving any puzzle though it is not necessarily the shortest or quickest for practical purposes. . . . 'Puzzle' involves 'capacity to be solved by some method or other.' " Most schoolwork, obviously, consists of the solution of puzzles posed for one reason or another by representatives of the adult community. The approaches to and techniques of puzzle solving are the principles and skills on which the student builds a capacity to solve other puzzles. All "arithmetic problems" are puzzles; indeed, all "problems to solve" in mathematics are puzzles, though "problems to prove" may be something else, on the highest levels of the art.

"Difficulties," Weldon continues, "are quite another matter. We do not solve them (though we sometimes talk loosely about 'The solution of the difficulty'), we surmount them, reduce them, avoid them, or ignore them. There may be all sorts of ways of dealing with them and getting out of them, but there is no demonstrably correct way. . . . The vicar may advise his parishoners as to their matrimonial difficulties but he cannot do their difficulties for them as he can do their crossword puzzles." As Weldon points out, a puzzle may look like a difficulty until the perplexed student discovers the method to employ. In absolute terms, however, the distinction between the puzzle and the difficulty is quite apparent. As Weldon puts it, "There are chess problems and bridge problems, but also unemployment problems and Negro problems. To use the same word in all these is to run a serious risk of practical error." It is this error, inherent in the stretching of the word "problem" that afflicts the social studies.

What is left to be covered by the word "problem" is the situation presented as given by the real world, and capable of verified solution through analysis into solvable puzzles. The sciences are full of such problems, though the most obvious examples are in applied science, where the engineer has the problem of designing the bridge and breaks it down into component puzzles. The facts are known, or can be accurately discovered; the results are accurately measurable. Rigorous criteria exist for the admission or exclusion of evidence.

Ambitious social scientists argue that their work will in fact reduce difficulties to problems, but the evidence so far is at best ambivalent—and in any case a set of fairly sophisticated puzzle-solving techniques, which high-school students do not have, is required before the job can even be attempted. In the schools, social "problems" are necessarily "difficulties." The problems themselves do not set boundary conditions, and students and teachers must go after them without developed criteria of relevance. What happens in the discussion is inherently miseducational.

Segregation is a difficulty; there may be a problem of caste, part of an anthropological system. Economic growth is a difficulty; there may be a problem of the allocation of resources. It is only by narrowing the focus that the teacher can winnow from brute reality the usable problem, and give life to terms like "problem solving." The means of maintaining the narrow focus are known in academic lingo as a "discipline."

Actions taken to overcome difficulties will of necessity be interdisciplinary, because reality is not to be encompassed by the focus of any one discipline. Teaching which fails to convey the limitations as well as the uses of a single discipline can hinder the formation of the synthesis implied in the choice of real actions. But one cannot *teach* the synthesis itself, only the boundary criteria and puzzle-solving techniques of the disciplines. Serious reform of social studies instruction, from the first grade through the new dispensations in the colleges, will require the abandonment of the "problem-solving" approach.

145

"CONTROVERSIAL ISSUES"

Even those who see all the theoretical and intellectual weaknesses of the problems approach sometimes like the Problems course, simply because it gives children a chance to examine with a somewhat colder eye than is customary the "controversial issues of our society." Fearful that today's young will be susceptible to tomorrow's demagogues, able men will sacrifice some chance at knowledge in the hope of securing immediate awareness.

"The foremost aim of instruction in high-school social studies," write Maurice Hunt and Lawrence Metcalf in their book *Teaching High School Social Studies,* "is to help students examine reflectively issues in the closed areas of American culture. . . . Teaching materials should be drawn from a selection of conflicting propositions in such controversial areas as race and minority group relations, social class, economics, sex, courtship and marriage, religion and morality, and national and patriotic beliefs, plus a wide range of relevant data to be used in testing them."

At Tufts, Franklin Patterson, a magnificently articulate Lasswellian political scientist, is giving a large chunk of his young life to promoting "an action approach" to the social studies in American schools. Ideally, Patterson would like to involve high-school students in many kinds of political and social action—ward working, doorbell ringing, handbill passing. Failing direct experience, he would like to use "open-end" case studies, preferably presented over television with maximum dramatic impact. His only opportunity to carry out his plans came in the summer of 1961, in Newton, with high-school students who physically cleaned up and rebuilt a community center, meanwhile reading vastly "in adult material, almost all of it ephemeral," and listening to talks by academicians, city planners, representatives of CORE, psychiatrists, etc. Patterson even gave them a unit on war, with a speech by an Air Force

146

officer, attacking Harrison Brown, and a careful analysis of what Kennedy did and did not say in his speech about Berlin that summer. How far Patterson could extend this approach beyond the confines of Newton and of summer sessions is anybody's guess, but it would certainly be interesting to watch him try. It would also be interesting to see how far the social-work component of the program would deviate from the old middle-class ideas of church or community service, as represented by the École Polytechnique (where the budding French Army engineers and intellectuals must spend two lunch periods a week visiting the poor) or the YMCA's McBurney School in New York (which, quite independently of its social-studies courses, sends boys to work at settlement houses and the like as part of its requirements for graduation).

At Rutgers, Donald Riddle, like Patterson a political scientist in his forties, is following a more conventional path to similar goals. McGraw-Hill has published a text for a Problems of Democracy course, by Riddle and his associates at the Eagleton Foundation, plus a book of readings designed to fit the text. There are also nine films of half an hour each, two of them case studies (one of Truman's seizure of the steel industry), the rest lectures; Riddle would have liked them all case studies, but Ford, which paid the bills, believes in lectures. "I've been married to the public schools for twenty years," Riddle says. "My wife is a first-grade teacher. For this course, I'm assuming the historical background; otherwise you never get beyond rudimentary history. I know a strong intellectual case can be made out for history only, but there aren't any historians trained to teach it, and I'm not sure the guild would permit them to teach it, anyway. I decided the thing to do was to stop talking and do something." Unlike Patterson, who is willing to work with reality plain, Riddle breaks his problems into areas of political science, economics, sociology, etc. But the emphasis is where Hunt and Metcalf want it—squarely on the big difficulties of the culture.

147

Anyone who cares about American education must be drawn emotionally by the invitation to ride with Hunt and Metcalf, Patterson and Riddle against the foul dragon of community ignorance and bigotry that devours so many of our schools. All over the country, retired policemen, military officers, and medical men, intellectually spoiled priests, sex-starved housewives, and little old ladies with umbrellas are snooping through the textbooks and soliciting tales out of school to prove that free public education (a socialist notion, anyway) makes Communists and perverts out of good little boys and girls. Not long ago, John Novotny wrote a story about a parrot who managed a prize fighter from a perch just behind the ring; and was, naturally, heckled by members of the crowd. He would reply to heckling with the ringing phrase, "Your sister goes up on the roof with Russians!" Some answer of this sort, but far nastier, has been routinized by thousands of ignorant vigilantes who feel obscurely that they are being heckled by teachers less parrot-minded than they are.

Incredible stories turn out to be true. In the city of Houston, for example, teachers are forbidden to mention the United Nations, because it is controversial. And elsewhere in Texas a school board member discovered that Bragdon & McCutchen on American history was subversive, because the cover was red and the cover design (an eagle clutching arrows and a scroll) could from a great distance be mistaken by an idiot Texan for a hammer and sickle. Recently, professors at the University of Washington had to go to the defense of a teacher threatened with dismissal as a Communist because he conveyed to students some relatively commonplace ideas about American industrial growth which had been stressed at a summer workshop for teachers at the university. In Indianapolis, the AFL-CIO supplied books and pamphlets to the high schools to balance the heavy inventory of Chamber of Commerce and NAM material already on school library shelves; a year later, not one of the union's contributions had actually been

148

forwarded from city headquarters to a school. (Not all the pressure, incidentally, comes from the right. There is also a kind of conspiracy afoot to deny the high crime rates of the immigrant and now Negro slums, to forget the ferocity and inhumanity of the Indian tribes that raped and looted on the prairies, to deny the undertone of violence and racketeering that accompanied much of the original organization of labor unions. The Scopes trial is not mentioned in any of the eight high-school American History texts that happen to be on my shelves; but, then, the McNamara Brothers aren't mentioned, either. If Aaron Burr had been a Catholic or a Jew or an Indian or a labor organizer, pressure groups would be insisting that Hamilton's death be presented as an unfortunate accident.)

Any attempt at curriculum reform in the social studies will get a fair number of teachers in political trouble with aggressive school boards and timorous superintendents. The grievance procedures of the National Education Association (the "defense committee") are usually not available to protect teachers in this kind of trouble, because the organization hates to embarrass superintendents, who are members, too. Any superintendent courageous enough to encourage NEA intervention will be courageous enough to protect the teacher by himself. College professors who wish to help with curriculum must also be ready to help with protection—perhaps to the extent of denying accreditation to high schools where teacher persecutions have occurred. A committee of the American Association of University Professors is already seeking ways to assure academic freedom to teachers at lower levels. One can imagine a future in which this committee would be the most active and the most heavily staffed branch of AAUP.

It is impossible to deny one's sympathy to teachers who must live at the mercy of powerful adults still unable to control their fear of the unknown. And the direct teaching of "controversial issues" is probably the best counterattack that can be made from

149

within the schools, because the great majority of Americans accept the utility of "objective" investigation and discussion of political and social disagreements. Nevertheless, I strongly believe that the temptation should be resisted. Controversy should never be shunned, but it should never be sought, either; gearing schoolwork to "controversial issues" will produce a poorly educated, and in many respects a miseducated, community.

Almost by definition, "controversial issues" are a source of sloganeering on both sides; and though society in its innards may know very well what the fight is about, the discussion is invariably unreal. The phenomena that underlie the politics are concealed by an exclusively ideational argument, and when information is adduced in support of a position it is usually irrelevant, marginal, or derivative from more profound causes which remain unexplored.

An example will serve better than philosophy. Not long ago, I took over a high-school class which had been wrestling with "inflation," a topic much in the newspapers and in political pronouncements. Inflation had been defined, as it almost always is, as a decline in the value of money, and public policy questions of various sorts had been discussed. Ignorance and incomprehension lay on the class like a fog, and in the forty minutes I had I tried what was for them (and for their teacher) a new path to the light. I do not give a verbatim transcript, partly because I have no notes, partly because I want to cheat, eliminating a number of faulty procedures on my part—the class was nowhere near this smooth. Basically, however, the approach was as follows:

—How do most people buy expensive things—houses, cars, washing machines, and so forth?

(On credit, the installment plan, buy-now-pay-later.)

—When people buy on credit, what sort of arrangement do they make with the seller?

(They pay it off so much a month.)

—Is it the same amount of money every month?

150

(Yes.)

—When people make this kind of deal, do they think it's going to be harder for them to make their monthly payments as time goes on?

(No.)

—What do they expect?

(They expect, probably, that it's going to be easier—that they'll get a raise or a promotion, and they'll have more money every month.)

—In other words, they're sure that money isn't going to be any harder to come by, for them—they hope it's going to be easier. Now, what are we talking about here?

And after a long delay, and many false starts, most of them into advertising, status seeking, etc., somebody came up with "Inflation." At this point, with one of the fundamental facts of economic life before us (the increasing downward inelasticity of wages in a developing capitalism), we could start talking as though the newspaper editorials had never been written, without "controversy." It will be observed, incidentally, that the difference between the debtor's and the creditor's attitude toward money is a recurrent theme in American history; if one could discuss the First Bank without Jefferson and Hamilton, the Second Bank without Jackson and Biddle, free coinage without Bryan and Hanna, the same relevance to contemporary affairs might be developed without direct discussion of "controversial issues."

On closer examination, Hunt and Metcalf's "closed areas" turn out to be less simple than they seem. Teaching in the "closed area" of "sex, courtship and marriage," for example, runs into the students' feeling that their teachers are unalterably square. (Hunt and Metcalf's statement that "sex is steadily opening as a field of reflective inquiry" would be regarded as positively cubic. Interestingly, in their discussion of the origins of American attitudes toward sex, these authors—who distrust history because it cannot supply

151

"if-then-always generalizations," as the statistical behavioral sciences supposedly can—fail to mention the violent change in customs brought by the introduction of *Spirochaeta pallida* to highly susceptible host organisms on the European continent around the year 1500.)

Other areas are not closed. "Social class" is a commonplace, though it is almost always seen in the puerile framework of magazine articles and Vance Packardisms. (Teachers also bring with them the simple-minded "upper-lower" stuff that dominates their educational sociology courses.) "Economics" is not barred, just ill-taught; and the naïve Keynesian doctrine that Hunt and Metcalf wish to introduce is not much less of a myth than the free-enterprise shibboleths that worry them. "Minority-group relations" and "national beliefs" are all over the curriculum, often enough in just the manner Hunt and Metcalf seem to approve (which can be nastily but not inaccurately called the You're-a-better-man-than-I-am-Gunga-Din approach). One should not label as "authoritarian" people whose first loyalties are to immediate family, spreading thereafter to friends, neighbors, tribe, etc.; the poor chaps are just human. Even if we could do it, we do not wish to create in the schools a community of saints.

The teaching of religious beliefs is so open an area that *Look* magazine builds circulation with it twice a year; criticizing religious beliefs, which Hunt and Metcalf seem to advocate, would be an outrageous invasion of privacy and a violation of the First Amendment when conducted in tax-supported schools. (The Supreme Court decision of 1962 touching on these matters, incidentally, is not "a controversial issue" to be argued over in schools; it is simply ludicrous to ask students for their "opinion" on whether the Supreme Court is right or wrong in its interpretation of the Constitution.)

Really "closed areas" are usually closed for damned good reason. One of the most immediate and unpleasant problems of American

152

slums is the brutality and dishonesty of the police—but what on earth is a school to teach about it? (Before reaching for an answer, readers might consider the long list of reasons why they would not wish their own sons to become cops working in a slum.) Again, despite much discussion of "American prestige" in history and problems classes, the roots of foreign distrust of the United States are never seriously examined. No American history text devotes as much as one percent of its bulk to the Philippine insurrection, the military interventions in Panama, Mexico, Cuba, Haiti, the Dominican Republic and the Soviet Union, all put together. The Mexican War is never seen as a classic grab of territory. The fact that it is only the United States which has used atomic weaponry (or napalm bombs) to kill people must be blotted out from discussions of the disarmament negotiations in the problems class, as it has been largely blotted out of the national consciousness. (So has all recollection of the Pilgrim Fathers praying for smallpox to strike the Indians even more severely.) Nor are these hypocrisies unfortunate. Children should think well of their country; and given the universal standards in these matters the United States has on the whole behaved over the years with great decency and generosity. On utilitarian grounds, too, it can be argued that a magnanimous self-image is more likely to make people magnanimous in the future. What purpose would be served by muckraking the history of American foreign policy? (Though, given a choice between this history and *The Ugly American*, which turns up on a number of reading lists, I would ardently recommend muckraking.)

Perhaps the most interesting of the "closed areas" is nuclear weaponry itself, a phenomenon which has produced enormous but as yet unexplored changes in the emotional climate of adolescence. Fear of death seems particularly pronounced in this age group, and children seem to live more than adults with a continuing sense of the threat of imminent destruction. Much of the panicky building of fallout shelters in American suburbs in 1961 seems to have been

153

stimulated by the children, who do not for a moment believe that the survivors will envy the dead. But "rational discussion" is hardly likely to diminish fear in this area.

Hunt and Metcalf are by far the most able spokesmen for the "controversies" approach and the Problems course; and their methods textbook is the only such worth reading. They raise a large number of questions which a teacher can actually put before a class, and point out a number of pedagogically useful contradictions between "typically American" beliefs. Even here, however, there is a great deal of opposing the good guys against the bad guys ("modern" against "traditional"), and a highly uncritical attitude toward social scientists who come up with what the authors regard as sound positions. In the end, their book demonstrates how much there is in heaven and earth undreamt-of in the philosophy of "controversy."

There is, of course, no reason why high-school students, as members of a community, should not take an interest in normal political life. Schools should encourage the formation of all sorts of political clubs—Young Democrats and Republicans, YPSLs and Young Americans, SANE, CORE. Any political debate that can be roused in school corridors (there probably cannot be much: adolescents are usually not all that interested in adult politics apart from the personality drama in elections) can inform the more disciplined work of the classroom and lift the sometimes perilously low level of liveliness at the school. We have—or should have—better things to do in the social studies class.

THE UNLUCKY: A DIFFICULTY

Ten percent of the population of the United States live with a visible mark of caste in the color of their skin; 25 percent or so of the remainder earn incomes so low that their life style is evident to the most casual observer. These people, somewhat to the horror

154

of much of the community, send their children, as the law requires, to the public schools—where, everyone knows, they make trouble. The American self image is and always has been (*see* Jefferson or Eisenhower) "independent" middle class, preferably yeoman; the first function of the schools is the acculturation of the young (the farm stays at the heart of the elementary curriculum in tribute to the self-image). Acceptance of the middle-class scale requires from the Negro an optimism his circumstances in this community do not warrant, and from the working-class child a rejection of the family background and the present pattern of his life—which is by no means so completely unsatisfying as most commentators on the schools seem to assume. Still, the child understands as well as the school that in American society (maybe in all societies) it is better to be middle class than to be poor; and Lord knows the Negro understands that it is better here to be white than to be colored. It is not only the schools that push the Negro and the working-class child toward acceptance of the white middle-class ethos; so-called "popular culture" in America is quintessentially middle-class. Only a fraction of these children will in fact make it to full participation in the middle-class community. But it can be argued that the degree of alienation from the mainstream which the others feel is determined in part by their experiences at school.

Teaching history and social science to what are now so properly called "culturally disadvantaged" children is an experience different from teaching such subjects to the heirs of the middle class. Negro children and slum children can, if the matter is called to their attention, regard these studies as central; they know they are in trouble, and they would like to know why. Unfortunately, the social sciences are themselves highly middle-class in orientation; they are the creation of capitalism, and their practitioners are overwhelmingly middle-class in origin. In dealing with lower-class life, they typically abstract away all that makes it worth living, and paint a picture so gloomy that most children will regard it as unreal

155

or unjust. When social scientists deal with slums, moreover, their information may be a good deal worse than that of slum children. (Hollis Caswell once "observed a study of housing in a school serving a community in which this was a real and important matter. The problem was selected for study for this reason. Students were greatly interested. But the conclusions that were reached were at variance with the findings of sociologists and of experts in housing." Caswell wrote these words in 1946; about a decade later, the "sociologists and experts in housing" caught up with the quality of information and insight in this slum class, and admitted they had been wrong.) Pretty-pretty history, the glorification of the middle class, its fight against feudalism and monarchy and militarism and robber barons, its construction of The Better Life for All, also cuts little ice with working-class and Negro children.

A much stronger case can be made out for the "problems" and "controversies" approach—particularly on the junior-high level—in schools populated largely by unlucky children, the very poor, the caste-oppressed, the remotely rural. Though they may know a great deal about their own situation that social scientists do not know, their world view is fearfully restricted. The first task of the school is to give these children what the New York system calls Higher Horizons, and the problems approach by its very simplicity allows them to move into a larger world. Trips and free-discussion sessions that produce intellectual delinquency in sophisticated middle-class students are more likely to stay honest in the slums. Panel reports and current-events programs can help these children become more articulate. Such "progressive" tactics, moreover, may break some of the prison atmosphere of the slum school, which typically operates under rigid discipline in halls, lunchrooms, and classrooms. (Among the more interesting experiments in this direction was Samuel Stratton's work at Chicago's Dunbar Vocational.) Hopefully, a few years of problem solving and discussion of controversial issues would leave a large fraction prepared to undertake more penetrating work in the disciplines.

Problems and controversies may also be a suitable tactic for the large group—one-third, in fact—which falls in the bottom third of the intelligence distribution. Moe Frankel, now of the Joint Council on Economic Education, reported a remarkable upswing of interest when he tried a pure problems approach—the problems chosen by the students, investigated through field trips and magazine reading, etc.—with the weakest classes at Scott High School in East Orange, N.J. W. R. Broderick stimulates unusual vitality in her classes at Louisville's Ahrens Vocational by similar procedures, controlling with forceful subtlety the topics that are chosen by the class groups.

Yet there remains in this corner a nagging suspicion that well-taught history will serve all but the least intelligent children better than even the best problems course. The slum child's initial freedom of interest, like his freedom of future, is far more limited than that of the middle-class child. But history is real, too, particularly in America, where everyone is where he is for relatively simple historical reasons. Starting from a base in the forces that put him where he is today, the slum child can learn a great deal of history, and form an interest in highly remote matters. For the Negro, American History pivots on the Civil War, World History on the rise and fall of colonialism; for the boy being trained in a vocational school, history pivots on the Industrial Revolution, seen in detail, as the source of current patterns. (Mrs. Broderick kept a large Ahrens group enthusiastic for months about the history of the labor movement.) Mystery and fear are far more likely to be removed from the ghost of the outside world when contemporary existence is seen as the product of a past rather than as a given phenomenon. And good teaching always makes history relevant.

From the classroom:

At Cleveland's Glenville High School, a small, crowded building set quite unpretentiously (for an American high school) in a neigh-

borhood once almost entirely Jewish, now almost entirely Negro.
(As a Negro teacher put it, not without bitterness, "We had our
ten years of integration, while the Jews were moving out and the
Negroes were moving in.") This is not, however, a slum school. No
place in America is positively good for a Negro, but Cleveland
seems to be about the least bad. The parents of many of these
students make a lower-middle-class income or better, the atmosphere
in Glenville's halls is as free as it is in Scarsdale's, and the attitude
toward education seems to have no more than the usual degree of
suspicion. Still, these children *are* Negro, part of an actively re-
pressed minority group. As seen on a very brief visit, Glenville
would seem to be considerable of an accomplishment. One history
class provided evidence that students here are learning more than
just social studies: when the teacher made reference to "The *Mar-
see-yay*," a mutter of "*Mar-say-yez*" rose from around the borders of
the room.

The teacher in this American History class is a hawk-nosed, lean,
crew-cut young man named Larry Cuban, a John Hay Fellow with
a personal devotion to history. He balances American History
around the Civil War for teaching purposes, but he does so out of
respect, not contempt, for his Negro students. He begins the class
by handing out "a very short reading list—on which there will be
no comments." Then he writes four names on the board:

> J. G. Randall
> Charles Beard
> Arthur Schlesinger, Jr.
> James Ford Rhodes

"We'll take these names to represent historians' views. You'll
remember Beard's thesis—'the clash between the Lords of the Lash
and the Lords of the Loom.' There were only 347,000 slave owners
in the South, 3,500,000 who didn't own slaves. Now, how many of
you would say slavery was the cause of the Civil War. Let's divide it

three ways here—Beardians, Stampps, and Fanatics. . . ." The class shows five Beardians, thirteen Stampps, and three Fanatics, with nine keeping their hands down.

"I know," Cuban says, "there are some of you who say, 'There's a little bit of each.' That's fine. My opinion is that it was slavery. You've got to remember, though, that the facts don't change—historians' opinions change. You have a glass of water; you can say it's half full or half empty, it's up to you."

A boy contributes, "I've read Olmsted, and I think he's right. It was a clash of nations. It wasn't economic, it was social."

"All right," Cuban says. "Now, I say I could have prevented the Civil War. With Lincoln's idea—what was that?"

A girl says, "Compensated emancipation."

"What does that mean?"

"Buy the slaves from the Southerners and set them free."

"Would it have worked? Would it have prevented the Civil War?"

The class groans, "No."

"Why not?"

A number of ideas are thrown forth—the Northerners didn't want to spend the money, you couldn't have set a price, the whole system was based on slaves. A girl says, "The Southerners wouldn't do it because it would make the Negroes equal to them."

"Let's get back to Beard," Cuban says. "Here. Less than ten percent of the Southerners owned slaves, but they all fought for slavery. How could they persuade the ninety percent to fight? You try it." He addresses two Negro girls and a Negro boy seated at his extreme left. "You're the slave owners. The rest of the class doesn't own slaves. You persuade them to fight for you."

One girl, giggling, tries, "Those Yankees, they want to come down and take everything away from you."

"Oh, no, they don't," Cuban says. "Just from you. I don't have anything they want."

159

"Our whole economy is based on slaves," says the boy.

"No, sir," says a boy in the non-slaveholding section, falling into the spirit of the situation. "My economy isn't. I got to do my own work."

The debate rages for a while, Cuban grinning over it, objecting where the 90 percent can't find a reply. "Come on, now," he says. "Why will these four million fight for four years? If you can't come up with this, class, the whole thing is completely unreal, just something in a textbook."

Finally, in the heat of the argument, one of the Negro girls in the slaveholding section comes up with, "Remember those slave rebellions? Remember what happened on those plantations? The Yankees will come down here and raise up those Negroes to be *your equals,* and there'll be no controlling them." The class roars with laughter at her, and she bends her head.

"Let's give it a name," Cuban says. He writes on the board, "WHITE SUPREMACY." He asks, "Any of you ever hear of U. B. Phillips?"

One boy has read it, and says, "He thinks that's the whole theme of Southern history."

The one white boy in the class, a West Virginia redneck, now makes his contribution: "You can find reasons all you like," he says. "I think they fought because they were told to fight."

Cuban says, "Maybe. Now, when we discuss Reconstruction, we'll find this same argument of White Supremacy used to justify . . . what? . . . anybody know?"

And a Negro boy says, "Segregation."

VI

*Are the Math
and Science Movements
a Model for Reform?*

"This was not, you understand, a *research* problem. It was merely a matter of taking known facts and putting them into teachable form."

—Bowen Dees of the National Science Foundation, discussing a program which trained people to teach the tricks of extraterrestrial navigation.

Ten years ago, people concerned about education in the United States were particularly worried by the quality and tone of math and science instruction. Math was notoriously the dullest and most unpopular subject in the high schools, and the college-bound student was felt to have done his duty if he undertook a rudimentary introduction to algebra and a set of Euclidean book proofs. In physics, most of the time was devoted to the definition of terms, the acquisition of "laws," and the solution of set problems in static mechanics (where students were typically advised to "use their rulers" to draw parallelograms of forces and then measure the lines to arrive at answers). Chemistry and biology were essentially exercises in classification. Introductory college courses in science usually assumed no prior knowledge—and, indeed, the assumption was hopeful, for the typical high-school course often did the student more harm than good.

Today the college math and science departments are busy revising their lower-level offerings, because rapidly rising numbers of entrants already know what used to be introductory college work, and have gone on to what were once second- or even third-level problems. Mathematical topics like spherical trigonometry, matrix algebra, probability, Cartesian geometry, and calculus are to be found in large numbers of high schools, and some students will have made the acquaintance of Boolean algebra and topology. The high-school physics course is now in many schools more sophisticated than what the colleges used to offer (to sophomores, usually, because so much of the freshman year was taken up with "general education"), and increasing numbers of high schools are moving into programs in biology and chemistry which give students a grasp of the real procedures as well as the descriptive vocabulary of the field.

Ten years ago, though math and science drew a highly intelligent small group of students, most of the best-prepared entrants to the more selective colleges and universities expected to specialize in the social sciences or literature; the colleges enforced for graduation a "science requirement" as well as a "language requirement" and a swimming certificate. Today the hierarchy of anticipated studies is reversed. The most highly qualified freshmen in the best colleges wish to major in math and science (the recent Brookings survey of enrollments went wrong by considering engineering a "science," which is not the view of college entrants or faculties). Indeed, one of the reasons social scientists are interested in the high schools is their reasoned envy of the physics department.

Many explanations can be given for the increasing reach and grasp of the science programs on both school and university levels. Obviously, outside forces—the rocket to the moon, the bomb big enough to kill us all, the job market, the Russians—have made

164

science courses more attractive to the adolescent community. Yet the last decade has also been a period of rapid increase in jobs for academicians in the social sciences. Industry and the foundations have found lucrative assignments for Ph.D.'s in psychology, sociology, economics, political science, anthropology. We have lived through the age of self-consciousness, of beatnikkery, of tax law, of advertising and mass culture, of existentialism and foreign travel. If today we had to explain a great rise of adolescent interest in social studies, we could do it easily in terms of "outside forces." Indeed, "attitude surveys" consistently show that high-school students are more interested in the material subsumed under "social studies" than in any other material—though typically they find their social studies courses the least interesting stuff at school.

This argument is offered strictly for purposes of illustration. If the market for instruction were wholly free, most children and adolescents would, I think, opt an education strongly biased toward science. Conscious of rising powers and ambitious for certainty, the adolescent is necessarily tugged toward studies where procedure counts for more than information, where irrelevancy can be squeezed out by logic, where a sometimes deceptive elegance brings startling new order to the disturbing chaos of sense experience. Yet the fact is that until quite recently traditional methods of teaching in mathematics and science blocked all but a few students from these rewards, and the math and science courses were unpopular. The dissimilar but still real rewards that adolescents might find in applying their powers to history or the social sciences are still blocked.

THE PSSC MODEL

The Physical Sciences Study Committee was launched a year before Sputnik, under the direction of Jerrold Zacharias of MIT, who had goaded James Killian, then president of MIT and later

165

head of President Eisenhower's Science Advisory Committee, into giving him the push to do the job. Further Zacharias-inspired pushing came from Alan Waterman of the National Science Foundation, which supplied the first funds and eventually, over a five-year period, put more than $7 million into the project. Other contributions came in from the Ford and Sloan Foundations, for specific purposes. Three key practical assumptions were explicit in the program:

1. That physics in a form wholly recognizable to working physicists could be taught on the high-school level;

2. That only the most extraordinarily talented of physicists and teachers would have the imagination and ability to create such a course;

3. That the only way to determine the viability of teaching materials was to teach them, and revise, and teach again, and remake, until finally you knew more or less what you were doing and why it worked when it worked.

From the beginning, the leaders of PSSC saw their job as extensive, complicated, and highly time-consuming. Writing a textbook would be only a fraction of the work, and not the most important fraction. Zacharias himself probably gave highest priority to the preparation of films which would show real scientists in real laboratories, explaining the real nature of important problems in physics. The films would "set the tone of the course," and they would have to be far superior to the usual educational (or educational television) material. PSSC set up its own studios and hired first-rank film talent at first-rank prices, and then worked, like the producers of Grade-A movies, on a 9-to-1 ratio, expecting to use only one of every ten feet of film actually shot.

PSSC began before the National Defense Education Act had made hundreds of millions of dollars of federal money available for high-school laboratories, and the scientists had to face up to the

166

fact that in most schools it was not possible to perform the experiments from which students could learn what they were studying. Filmed experiments, while helpful, would not replace the experience of fiddling with the realia. Zacharias and his colleagues therefore designed a score of pieces of inexpensive laboratory equipment —micro-balances made from soda straws, cheap stroboscopes and the like, requiring no more than flat surfaces, electric wiring, and running water—which could be sold as a package both to ill-equipped and conventionally-equipped schools.

Though PSSC aimed to break the highly verbal patterns of instruction in physics, and insisted from the beginning that it was *not* the group that measured highest on IQ tests which would perform best in the new course, its creators were themselves literate men with a strong belief that people can learn from reading, too. The ultimate textbook (built from four separate pamphlet-sized "units" written by different people) was to be a guide and a source of interesting problems. To accompany it, the committee chose or commissioned or wrote some seventy-five books of supplementary readings, to be published in paperback form as the Anchor Science Study Series.

Finally, PSSC recognized that no material is, was, or could be teacher-proof. The physicists ran summer institutes, more of them every year, to train teachers. By the end of 1962, nearly twenty-five hundred teachers—who come in contact with perhaps a quarter of a million students each year—had spent at least one summer working on the PSSC course.

The personnel to staff this effort were chosen mostly by Zacharias himself, and ruthlessly sloughed off by Zacharias if their work failed to meet his standards. Using his own prestige, that of his institution, and that of his friends, Zacharias dragooned into work for the high schools one hundred of the outstanding physicists in the United States. "Writing groups" at MIT, Harvard, Cornell,

167

Bell Labs, and Illinois (where Max Beberman's VICSM math had paved the way) devoted their summers and parts of their winters to thinking up ideas and angles for high-school physics.

Neither Zacharias nor his colleagues believed that they knew enough to construct an "ideal" physics course. What they were after was a very good physics course that could be taught in high schools. Physicists who were not also teachers (Zacharias himself had always taught a part of the MIT introductory course) could offer little to the PSSC effort, and the committee felt a desperate need for high-school teachers who were also physicists. A nation-wide talent search uncovered, with difficulty, a handful of teachers who could function in tandem with the handful of top-level university physicists working on PSSC. Feedback from actual teaching experience was regarded as essential. And the most nearly indispensable members of the PSSC working group were the men with a gift for seeing why students didn't learn something and how new traps could be laid; the heroes here were Philip Morrison of Cornell, David Page of Illinois, and especially the late Francis Friedman of MIT, who edited the final draft of the textbook and acted as Zacharias's scholarly conscience and balance wheel throughout the enterprise. As the summer institutes proceeded and the number of teachers who understood the material increased, PSSC was able to secure increasingly valid information on the quality of its efforts.

At no time did the scientists place any great weight on "scientific measurements" of what they were accomplishing. They did work with the Educational Testing Service to design a test to assure that PSSC students would not be penalized in the bureaucratic world of college admissions and to guarantee themselves against gross overoptimism about what they were accomplishing. But impressionistic, intuitional feedback from those who were teaching and learning the material weighed much more heavily than test results when the committee sat down to analyze how it was doing. The committee is still analyzing and revising, on the basis of judgment. The question of quality has always been first in the physicists'

168

minds; as accomplished men in a technical field, they have never doubted their ability to recognize a high order of quality when they see it.

PSSC was lavishly financed, and could pay the people who worked on it more than they would receive from their universities for equivalent time—though still substantially less than they could get from private industry for consulting work. What has kept the program going for more than six years, however, is neither the pay nor the sense of the importance of the job, but the fascination which masters of a discipline feel when they seriously undertake the intellectual exercise of looking at their field afresh, through the eyes of the beginner. Normal intellectual work occurs within a framework of conventions so long accepted and so casually employed that the scholar forgets not only the means of their acquisition but also their ultimate significance. Looking at physics as an intelligent adolescent sees it, the physicists found much that was interesting, and a little that was important, with reference to their own work. Significantly, several of the physicists, led by Friedman, moved down to work in the elementary school once the superstructure was up and the scaffolding removed in the high-school courses.

Nobody in physics would argue that the PSSC course is the only, or even necessarily the best way to teach the subject. Zacharias himself never wished to prepare a physics course: in his original scheme, he wanted a full-size science program which would break down what he regarded as artificial barriers between physics and chemistry and eventually between both and biology. This procedure proved impractical in early meetings, and was regretfully dropped, but it is now being revived, by the National Science Foundation, under the cryptic label "Phase 2." NSF, with the full blessing and encouragement of Zacharias, will also support another physics course, aimed at the engineering-minded rather than the science-minded in the adolescent community.

Taking PSSC as a point of reference (sometimes for purposes

of disagreement), and taking financial and administrative assistance from the National Science Foundation, the mathematicians, chemists, and biologists set to work in committees to reform instruction in their own disciplines on the secondary level. A unified study committee of biologists has produced three separate high-school courses; two committees of chemists have produced a course each; and several groups of mathematicians have developed new approaches to the six years of secondary-school math. At present no fewer than five groups under the leadership of university mathematicians are working on materials for elementary-school math, a subject they have already made far more extensive than mere arithmetic. All these groups have proceeded more or less according to the model established by PSSC, creating and trying out new text, laboratory, and supplementary materials, and training teachers in the use of these materials through narrowly purposeful summer institutes. They have involved themselves in actual teaching to varying degrees—but all have assumed that the essence of the job was finding ways to teach the subject, not merely determining (or justifying) the goals of instruction.

THE THEORY BEHIND THE MODEL

It has been delightful in dry years to watch the mathematicians and scientists, largely ignorant of the history and theory of education, develop painfully and piece by piece an educational philosophy superficially similar to that of the early progressives at the turn of the century. Education, they argued, had to be active; an ounce of discovery was worth a pound of rote; the physics course was not preparation for physics, it was physics itself. Talk is cheap; the ability to handle definitions does not necessarily imply the ability to perform. What the child learns is not necessarily the thing you think you are teaching. The energy in the classroom is the energy of the assembled students, and the function of teaching is to release this energy in productive channels, not to impart wisdom. The mathematicians and scientists found that they learned from teaching, that aiming the program at the child did not necessarily water down its content but might in fact distill its essence from conventional irrelevancies. Whatever else the math and science reform movements accomplished, they unquestionably gave a number of highly intelligent and powerful men a view of education far more sophisticated than the view held by any other group of similar intelligence and power since the early years of this century.

Yet the work done by the mathematicians and scientists has rested on theoretical foundations in part original with them, and never fully stated, though Jerome Bruner touched interestingly upon the matter in his book *The Process of Education*. If the math and science movements are to be taken as models for work in other disciplines, these theoretical foundations must be understood, and their practical implications realized, by the people who are to make the attempts. The theory can be simplified, not unfairly, into two assumptions, an argument, and a conclusion:

First Assumption: The real world is really there. Like the scientist-philosophers (Russell, Whitehead, Jeans, etc.) whose writings spread through the general intellectual community during the heyday of progressivism, the new scientist-educators have a cold answer to questions of epistemology. Different people see the same meter readings, and experiments are duplicable. An optical illusion is demonstrably an illusion. If reality is asked a good question, over and over again, it will give the same answer, within a statistically predictable range, over and over again; where the answer varies unpredictably, the question is no good. All real disagreements can be empirically resolved, eventually—though as yet, the scientists insist, we know very little.

Second Assumption: On some basic operational level, all human learning (including perception) involves the same process. Every

171

learning theory is of course based on this assumption; indeed, behaviorist theories tend to assume that human and animal learning are identical. The scientists, however, are natural Gestalt psychologists, because so much of what is most interesting in the history of a science seems to have occurred by intuitional jump rather than by trial and error. The primary question to them is the organization of raw experience by the learner (or by the discoverer, who is, of course, merely the first learner).

Argument: Now, if all learning follows the same process, and the real world is really there, every wholly naïve human intelligence (a theoretical construct impossible in reality) would organize each wholly new experience in the same way. In less elaborate language, there *is* such a thing as common sense; given no background or identical backgrounds, the commonality of mankind would draw from the same experiences the same beliefs about reality. These isotropic beliefs, however, tend to be mistaken: reality is far more complicated than common sense will say it is. To handle reality, mankind has developed scholastic disciplines, which depart, often radically, from common sense. Education, whenever it is more than initiation into the myths and rituals of the tribe, is the induction of the learner into these disciplines. Bruner is insistent on this point, demanding that all education reflect "the structure of the discipline." And from this argument there flows a further:

Conclusion: The difficulties of learning are inherent in the material to be learned. If the generality of mankind finds difficulty in mastering an experimentally verified explanation of reality—and human learning is essentially the same for all individuals, and the real world is really there—it can only be because raw experience misleads common sense. Teaching, then, is the reorganizing of raw experience in such a way that the human mind will discover the usable patterns of thought called disciplines rather than the hodgepodge of irrelevancies called common sense.

Given the theoretical schema, the scientist can reduce the problem of improving education down to two manageable parts:

172

1. He can construct pedagogic models (systematic reorganizations of experience, ripple tanks for wave motion in physics, black boxes for the essence of the experimental approach in chemistry), from which learners will by normal processes induce the usable discipline. This task, it will be observed, is wholly empirical; as long as the scientist assumes that all human learning occurs the same way, he does not need to know how it occurs. The value of the pedagogic models he develops can be experimentally determined: students either do or do not tend to induce the discipline from the model. Much the same attitude, by the way, lies behind programed instruction, which accounts for the *Angst* toward programing felt by the mathematicians and scientists, who do not get along very well with Skinnerian psychologists but feel that there simply must be something here which they can use.

2. He can train teachers specifically to work with these models. Teachers will still, of course, require considerable background in the discipline; otherwise they will not understand the value of the models and they will introduce common-sense material which appears to be but in fact is not relevant to the models. The better educated the teacher is, the more easily he will handle the model. But the training of teachers, beyond education, must be based, as it has not been, on the materials they will take with them into the classroom—and a great deal can be accomplished with decently educated teachers by an intensive summer's work narrowly directed toward the successful employment of quality materials.

Fighting the flood of this argument, educators will often clutch, as at a life raft, on to Dewey's division of educational efforts as either "logical" (directed toward the discipline) or "psychological" (directed toward the child). But the strength of the scientists' approach is that it is both logical and psychological. Though it seeks as an end result the logic of the discipline, it does not attempt (as the Herbartians and, for that matter, the Progressives sometimes did) the direct teaching of the logic. Instead, it seeks to match experiences with the psychology of learning in such a way that the logic will emerge. Indeed, the best of the scientists have learned from their teaching that their own view of the clearest and simplest presentation of an idea is often misleading—that if they are to teach successfully, they must somehow find out what the idea means to someone who never ran into it before.

But within the other disciplines, able men, some of whom have actually thought about education, feel queasy at the prospect of adopting the scientists' model as a pattern for reform movements in history and the social sciences. What seems to be bothering them can be sketched in the framework of the scientists' theory:

THE OBJECTIONS TO THE THEORY

To the scientists' first assumption, that the real world is really there, the historians and even some of the social scientists reply nervously that in their terms reality is hard to define. When one must deal with words and deeds (let alone music and art) rather than with meter readings and mathematical symbols, reality seems to be what can be found in the mind of the beholder. Asked the same good question, reality will give different answers from culture to culture and from time to time. One man's fish, as the late Joe Palmer once pointed out, is another man's *poisson*.

To the scientists' second assumption, that all learning involves the same process on some operational level, most historians and social scientists reply, in effect, "Who cares?" They believe that prior learnings (acquired ways of viewing experience, existing "phase assemblies" in the brain, to use D. O. Hebb's terminology) will be more important than this invisibly distant process in determining what the individual sees when he looks at the world—and prior learnings vary greatly from person to person, even at an early age. Every teacher has had the experience of presenting the same material the same way to two different classrooms of students—and watching it produce two very different sets of results. As teachers,

174

of course, the scientists know this problem. Some of them will argue that if the child is caught young enough (in elementary school) the disparity among prior learnings can be controlled; some will contend that the ideal pedagogic model can cut across prior learnings and even across great differences in individual ability and classroom psychology; some will accept the difficulty but insist that teaching must deal with only a finite and probably small number of erroneous prior learnings, and a manageable number of pedagogic models will turn the trick. Social scientists, accustomed to the nasty habits of unknown variables, trapped every so often by elements in their disciplines which turn out to be *inferior* to common sense, fear that the differences introduced by prior learnings will be too various and too great to be controlled by straightforward analysis of the contact between students and material.

If the real world exists at least in part in the mind of the beholder, and human intelligence reacts to experience largely on the basis of varying prior learnings, then the difficuties of learning are largely inherent in the individual rather than in the material to be learned.

But from this argument there follows, unfortunately, nothing to do. The teacher in the classroom cannot look to the masters of a discipline to help him; he is stuck with his intuition and with the ludicrous guidance given by long, pompous, quasi-religious statements of the "goals of instruction" in the social studies.

EASY ANSWERS TO HARD QUESTIONS

The dichotomy is, of course, oversimplified and overstated. The participants in the dialogue are brought together by the fact that the scientists have accomplished something in the schools, and the other scholars would like to accomplish something, too. The problems the two groups face are enough alike in important aspects so that similar procedures may make sense, despite divergent theories. Materials and methods are common to all education; the scientists,

175

whatever one thinks of the theory, have developed ways of improving both materials and methods.

Perhaps the most serious difficulty in any academic instruction, scientific or otherwise, is to get down below the verbiage (which most children can memorize, if prodded hard enough) to the processes which the words symbolize. Getting at the reality of the conservation of matter or the development of vertebrates or the periodic tables may not be, as a teaching matter, all that different from getting at the phenomena behind Progressivism or Marginal Analysis or the Protestant Ethic—or, for that matter, the language behind the grammer. To give the word and then the example, which was the customary procedure in science instruction before the scientists let loose and is still the customary procedure in the social studies, is known to be a highly ineffective way to teach, and it survives only because of the severe shortage of pedagogic models from which children can induce for themselves the idea behind the word.

If only because reality itself is blurred, and because irrelevancy (not to mention inaccuracy) constantly intrudes from the pervasive common sense of the culture, the construction of pedagogic models in the social studies will be far more difficult than it is in science. But it has, after all, been done—in the Bible, by Plato and Aristotle, by Hobbes and Locke and Hume, by Adam Smith and Karl Marx and Sigmund Freud. The power of Aristotle's thought over two millennia derived largely from the excellence of his pedagogic models. Beard's thesis on the makers of the American Constitution still looms large in the schools, though historians no longer credit it, because it serves so well as a pedagogic model. Books like *The Lonely Crowd* and *Patterns of Culture* dominate introductory courses, to the distaste of most sociologists and anthropologists, because, to hammer on the ugly phrase, they work so well as pedagogic models.

How far others can follow the mathematicians and scientists in adopting an inductive approach is still an open question. Induction,

176

or "heuristic," as the mathematicians and scientists practice it, is a process of successive approximation. A child need not be told that his answers are right or wrong, because he can feed them back into the problem himself, see how they work out, and hunt around for the reasons for error. The scientists, moreover, make heavy use of analogy, which is more complicated in its effects when the subject under consideration is less simple.

By approaching their subject through the disciplines, by breaking reality into pieces with defined parameters, social studies teachers can undoubtedly follow a far more inductive approach than they do today. Some are already trying it—young Richard McCann of Newton's Meadowbrook Junior High defines teaching as "a game of trying to structure the situation so students will feel they are coming out with their own conclusions." But only people who are truly learned in the disciplines to be taught are likely to come up with those uniquely organized slices of reality that allow the student to feed back his own answers. Most teachers are no better equipped to make such slices for themselves than they are to invent original experiments for students to try out in the labs.

Even in the hands of the most superbly skilled math and science teachers, induction does not work equally well with all children in all classrooms. Less intelligent children, almost by definition, handle induction less well—though the method quickly reveals that children who do poorly in the usual learn-and-apply-the-formula pattern are not necessarily the less intelligent. Most classrooms can be made to buzz with excitement in the hands of, say, a David Page or a Robert Davis, the two most spectacularly skilled reformers of elementary arithmetic instruction, but they have failures, too, for reasons they cannot always locate. It is not impossible that differences in individual ability and prior learnings, and differences in the psychology of the class as a whole, will show up even more strongly in the more value-laden areas of the social studies. Still, you never know till you try.

The three strongest blocks to reform are the reluctance of major

177

scholars to take the time from their own work and to see themselves as educators of children, the lack of intellectual sophistication among people in positions of power in the educational hierarchy, and the total inadequacy of teacher preparation.

Of the three, the least formidable at this writing is the reluctance of the scholars. Partly because of the example set by the mathematicians and scientists, partly because the idea of working with younger children is intrinsically fascinating, partly because they are irritated by what passes for their life's study in current high-school programs, the scholars in increasing numbers are ready to devote considerable time to working with teachers and children on valid school instruction.

The superintendents and their allies in the administration of the education departments are a more serious handicap. Their prestige rests in large part on their assertion that they know what children can learn, and the proposition that children can acquire analytical skills greater than their own is as distasteful to them as it is to the normal run of adults. They seem permanently wedded, moreover, to the notion that reality is what meets their eyes; and it is far easier for physicists to convince them that atoms are as real as pulleys and levers than for economists, say, to convince them that imputed income is as real as installment interest. Philosophically, too, they are almost to a man adherents to Dewey's monism, to the notion that all knowledge is revealed by "the scientific method"; and their inexperience with speculation permits them to keep their faith in scientific method while accepting the new slogan about "the structure of the discipline," which clearly implies that there are as many ways of knowing as there are differentiated disciplines. (One of the dangers in the present situation is that the "scientific" sociologists, who share a monistic view, will join with the educators to dominate curriculum revision.) Nevertheless, superintendents and administrators do not really *care* much about philosophy, and most of them have learned through their political career to be a modern version of the Vicar of Bray: if the wind blows hard enough, they will bend with it.

Teacher preparation is the worst impediment, and the only sign of hope here is the relative success the National Science Foundation has had with its summer institutes and workshops. Teacher training as the scientists have conceived it rests on prior preparation of the actual materials to be taught. If one can put into the teacher's hands the stuff he will actually take with him into the classroom, one can give him specific help in making the material work. Conventional teacher training in the United States has virtually no point of contact with this procedure. Many different sets of materials are available for most courses that a teacher may be asked to teach, and the choice among them is bureaucratically made for a school or a school system. Because a teacher will not have the opportunity to choose the materials with which he works, training institutions have felt themselves unable to offer specific methods based on the books and pamphlets and films and recordings to which the student will be exposed. This year's graduates from the teacher-training institutions are about as ill equipped to teach the new math and science material as their predecessors over a decade ago—everybody still has to be retrained at a summer program.

Teacher preparation in the United States is insufferably generalized. It rests on observation—usually superficial observation—of what good teachers seem to do. Thus, since most good teachers are ingenious at pointing out the relevance of a study to what is in today's papers, teacher-training institutions build a philosophy around contemporaneity; since most good teachers know through peripheral vision the social relations and psychological difficulties of their students, teacher-training institutions offer techniques of sociodrama and psychodrama by which imperceptive teachers are supposed to be able to find out what gives in the buried life of the classroom. Emphasis has been placed precisely on those areas where technique cannot replace insight; and the areas where technique is valid, in

179

the presentation of material to be learned, have been almost completely neglected.

This pattern cannot be broken overnight, because nobody has done the fundamental research on student reactions to specific material. (And school superintendencies have not yet been persuaded, or forced, to permit teachers to choose their own materials, as they do in France.) Any careful preparation of new materials for classroom use, however, must involve just this sort of research in how students react to the teaching of each aspect of a subject. Thus improvements in teacher training rest, over the long run, on the preparation of materials by teams of highly intelligent and highly observant scholars and teachers. Systematic investigation has been made possible in the last few years by the development of programed instruction, the first really valuable research tool education has ever had. We will know what we can teach, and how to teach it, only after new materials are prepared. It may turn out that special temperamental as well as intellectual requirements must be met by prospective teachers—the inductive approach, for example, obviously demands a degree of patience as well as a depth of knowledge not often encountered. Teaching is always going to be hard work for those who do it well.

Meanwhile, teacher education and teacher training must be considered together, not as two separate pieces of a college schedule. To handle PSSC, teachers had to learn considerable physics—but they learned it through detailed consideration in depth of what they would present to their students. Teacher training based on the materials to be taught will inevitably involve extensive learning of the subject. It can be argued, indeed, that the best way to learn about, say, the origins of the Civil War, is to find answers for all the questions students might ask about it (for the purpose, naturally, of helping students discover such answers for themselves, not for the purpose of telling them). Some of the academic specialization now expected of secondary-school teachers (and soon, one hopes,

180

to be expected of all teachers) can probably be accomplished through extended, realistic "methods" courses tied directly to the material to be taught.

Yet one would not wish to separate too soon or too drastically the prospective teacher from the prospective scholar (or, indeed, the prospective amateur) of a discipline. And there could be useful references for future teaching at any level in a college professor's intelligent presentation of a college course. Ideally, one would wish any teacher to consider himself a student first, and a "professional" only later. Even if teacher training is made a good deal more educational than it is today, teachers ultimately will require—and are, indeed, entitled to receive—a college education far more carefully considered, imaginatively taught and intellectually respectable than anything they are likely to get at most (not all) American institutions of "higher education" today.

Reform of secondary instruction and teacher training presupposes at some point in time reform of the colleges, still, on the average, despite great improvement during the last decade, the weakest section of the American educational effort.

Appendices

APPENDIX A

Professional Content: Brief Historical Background of Some American Institutions, in the Reference Frame of Political Theory

In political theory, what the commonality of mankind asked from governments was that law should be reasonable and should be applied equally to all supplicants before it; and that taxes should not eat up for the benefit of authority the fruits of man's labor. Thus, the good prince dealt justice to his people and ideally lived on the proceeds of his own estates, plus whatever he could seize abroad.

Yet the prince, embodying in his person the symbol of the community, is a kind of god, or, at the least a god's vicar. It was not in the competence of the commonality, or even of the nobility, to say that the laws were unreasonable or the burdens excessive: the king could do no wrong. Someone could kill him, however (or, in the charming custom of Byzantium, blind him), at which point he would no longer be king and even the most serious theorist would have to admit that the argument was moot. Accomplished, the act was legitimate. Somewhere there had to be law higher than the king's law; the Chinese developed the doctrine of the Mandate of Heaven given to rebels against a bad ruler, and in Catholic Europe a Pope could in theory dissolve the bonds of obligation that held a people to their sovereign.

Teachers, historians, and social scientists all have a fondness for this "higher law" approach to the world, and in various guises ("Teutonic superiority, Manifest Destiny, dialectical materialism, white supremacy, the wave of the future, the decline of the West) it comes forward periodically to justify enormities quite as arbitrary as the whim of kings. "Higher laws" are essentially anarchic because everyone may have his own; they shake the sovereign without securing the subject. In sixteenth-century England, after Edward II's descendants had killed themselves off in the Wars of the Roses, their dubious successors subjected the community to repeated doses of the final abuse of royal authority, soon to be known by the phrase *cujus regio, ejus religio.* In defense against the throne of an immensely popular monarch, the gentry of England, not knowing what they were doing, invented the argument to which kings could make no answer. The king ruled by divine right, the king could do no wrong; but the king was bound to observe the customs of his country, the king could not by his own single will interfere with what had been done in the land, "the memory of man runneth not to the contrary." The Elizabethans invented "the liberties of the subject," granted to be sure by the sovereign, but granted as a matter of course. Precedent was above the king, and the community reserved to itself, through Parliament, the interpretation of Precedent. Elizabeth never believed it for a minute, but her subjects did. Through the debates of her Parliaments runs this thread of sincere but preposterous assertions of precedent, to justify outrageous novelty.

Gradually, over one long reign, the Royal Prerogative was worn away by the growth of asserted custom. In the name of custom, Englishmen were soon by Bill of Attainder to force a king to kill his own first minister; and then to kill the king himself. Presently, despite the theorizing of Hobbes, this was seen to be a mistake (it went against Precedent). Eventually, the solution was found, and a century of political agitation was ended by inviting to the throne a king who was pledged to protect "the liberties of Englishmen." By then, custom and precedent, sometimes very remote precedent, had been exalted to the Stoic status of "natural law."

Now there were Englishmen living on the American continent; and soon they too were to demand the rights that Englishmen had possessed, "the memory of man runneth not to the contrary." Occupants of a rich new land, from which smallpox was clearing the aboriginal inhabitants at a most satisfactory rate, they had no customs of their own, and they boned up on the precedents of the mother country. Fundamental laws touching on the rights and equities of persons could not be altered by the king alone—and could not be altered even by the king-in-Parliament, if the people affected by the act were not somehow represented in the Parliament. Legal casuistry backed at every step the anger of men who felt themselves ill-used. The founders of the American Republic were less the remote heirs of Locke than the immediate descendants of Blackstone; Burke warned the king not to pick quarrels with colonies where every literate man was a lawyer. Arguing that circumstances alter cases—a doctrine directly contradictory to Blackstone—a stupid ministry forced war on the colonists. Driven to the full, radical statement of what had been felt as a conservative position (throughout the long struggle between king and Commons it had always been maintained, sincerely if wrongly, that the king was the one attempting innovations), Jefferson denied that there was any inherent authority in kingship: "governments derive their just powers from the consent of the governed."

Left finally to themselves, the Americans chose constitutional, representative democracy—which their leaders, on good evidence, considered a highly aristocratic form of government. The power of the people's representatives was to be hedged with constitutional restrictions, to assure that the will of the populace did not create a tyranny worse than monarchy. Much of the Constitution and nearly all the Bill of Rights, which had to be added to it to get it passed, simply enumerate the acts of a British king which an elected American government would not be permitted to follow. The document is a masterpiece of legal draftsmanship, containing only two technical errors (those who have forgotten them are referred to the Eleventh and Twelfth Amendments). How far its proscriptions merely enshrined Precedent, the rule of the common law, was soon a matter of debate; inevitably, it was the law courts, set up as an independent branch of government, which undertook to resolve such debates to determine what was meant by the "due process of law" required of any governmental action touching on life, liberty, or property, to make rational the working relationship between sovereign states and a federal government. Marshall's extension of the apparent

187

power of the court appeared so remarkable a feat because it occurred against a background of swelling popular democracy, the appearance of "the kingly commons," the elimination of property requirements for the franchise, the election to office of people who would need the emoluments of office to support their families. Yet, despite the deliberate vagueness of the "exceptions" which the Constitution allowed in the relations between Congress and the Court, the importance Marshall asserted for his branch of government was always present in the document. In part, the revolutions of England and America had been fought for the security of *stare decisis*. "Scarcely any question arises in the United States," Tocqueville wrote, "that is not resolved, sooner or later, into a judicial question."

The doctrine of judicial review is the great American contribution to political theory. The courts guarantee that pre-established rules and customs will not be violated in the creation and application of law. Orders issue from appellate courts to strike down the law, dismiss the case, free the prisoner. But this protection deals only with form: the appellate judge does not assert a wisdom superior to that of the legislature, the original judge or the jury. His personal beliefs are, ideally, irrelevant; he speaks as the servant of the law. Thus it was possible for a Justice Holmes, doubting the effectiveness of most social legislation, to argue that the states had a right to try. And it is possible for people who agree whole-heartedly with the results of Brown et al. v. Topeka Board of Education to feel uncomfortable with the opinion, on the grounds that the Fourteenth Amendment does not enact Mr. Gunnar Myrdal's *American Dilemma* any more than Mr. Herbert Spencer's *Social Statics*.

In these terms—and *only* in these terms—a case can be made out for the silly commonplace that "we have a government of laws, not of men."

APPENDIX B

Examples of Errors and Miscalculations in the

Task Force Report on Economic Education

EXAMPLE 1:
Page 14: "One of the essential lessons of economics is that we cannot have our cake and eat it, too."

Oddly enough, one of the essential lessons of economics is that you are not going to have your cake unless you are prepared to eat a large part of it. As the report itself points out thirty-eight pages later, "A satisfactory growth in output requires a satisfactory growth in spending." Whether it is called overproduction or underconsumption (or, in the fashionable new language, "excessive inventory accumulation"), the presence of too many unsold goods on the shelf is the proximate cause of recessions and declines in capital investment.

The Task Force economists are stuck with their cake because they demand the concept of "scarcity" as the beginning of study about economics. Meno Lovenstein of Ohio State recently told Ohio school administrators that the great difficulty about teaching economics was the need to start with a generalization like scarcity. (These same administrators had recently been made the victims of a Scope and Sequence Chart from a Joint Council workshop, complete with a glossary by the chairman of the economics department at Ohio University, including definitions like "Inflation: A disproportionate rise in the general price level when the economy is at full employment"; and "Capital: One of the major factors of production consisting of property from which an income is derived, expressed in terms of money.") There

189

is no disposition here to argue the case for "the economy of abundance"; but it must be recognized that scarcity as a central concept can be made to work only if leisure time or the maintenance of some other tribal custom (most spectacularly, the Hindu reverence for the cow) is regarded as a scarce economic good. Insistence on "scarcity" as the center of economics is not necessary; "choice" implies all the scarcity the economist needs as a foundation for his study. To start with "the wants" of the members of a society, as the Task Force does, is to plunge economics immediately into problems of anthropology, sociology, and psychology where the economist has, to say the least, no special competence.

EXAMPLE 2:
Pages 23-24: "The concept of opportunity (or alternative) cost is a central one. If resources are used to satisfy one want, they cannot be used to satisfy another. Thus, the alternative use that is not met is, in a real sense, the cost of satisfying the want for which the resource *is* used. For example, labor or machinery used to manufacture typewriters cannot be used at the same time to produce bicycles . . . A hundred dollars spent on a new suit may mean forgoing a new stove for the kitchen."

This argument is the heart of the economist's habit of mind. (It also includes all the "scarcity" anybody needs.) But the examples chosen are so obvious as to make the point seem trivial. For business, the startling thought is that the costs of spending retained income for expansion are roughly the same as the costs of borrowing the money to finance the expansion (a fact Roger Blough, among others, apparently never discovered), because the retained earnings could be loaned at interest if they were not expended here. For the individual, the fact is that his home ownership costs him, in addition to the mortgage and tax and maintenance payments he knows all about, the interest he could be earning on the money he has sunk in the house. (In Britain, the rental value of a man's home is part of his taxable income.) It is where an economist's view goes *against* common sense, not where it reinforces common sense, that non-economists are likely to learn something. The example of the $100 suit vs. the $100 stove, by the way, is a disturbing case of professorial perception. Apart from college professors, most

190

Americans spend much less than $100 for a suit, and more than $100 for a stove. It does not seem wholly unreasonable to ask that economists should know such things.

EXAMPLE 3:
Pages 24-25: "All economic systems (capitalist, communist, or any other) face the same basic economic problems. . . . It is important to recognize that while different economic systems set their goals and manage the allocation of their resources very differently, in many respects they differ only in degree as to how they solve their economic problems."

Systems do not face or solve problems; people face and solve problems, and the result of their actions is called a system. The objection here is not purely semantic. Most students (indeed, most adults) have a much exaggerated view of the degree to which their actions are free. The notion that systems solve problems is closely related to the notion that people "choose" systems, an idea which inhibits serious study.

EXAMPLE 4:
Page 30: "Students should also understand, in broad terms, the *principle of diminishing returns*. This principle states, crudely, that when more of one productive resource (for example, labor) is combined with a fixed amount of another (for example, natural resources) under any given state of technology, the output per unit of the first will after some point diminish. . . . Students should also see that this law can be offset by improvements in technology." (A footnote here suggests that "more precise analysis is desirable for superior students, but a rough statement can serve a useful general purpose for most students.")

"Diminishing returns" is a phrase from the eighteenth century, and it is intrinsically misleading today because the word "returns" has come to be synonymous with profit. The "law" is actually one of increasing marginal cost. Why the Task Force chose to eliminate the concept of the margin from its version of the introductory college course is one of the mysteries of the report. G. Leland Bach, chairman of the Task Force, writes in a letter that working economists find "average cost" a more fruitful measure than "marginal cost," which is no doubt true. (Businessmen know their average costs, not their marginal cost.) But one of the contributions economists make to businessmen, as

Sidney Alexander of MIT pointed out in a Brookings lecture, is their stress on the fact that maximum profit does not mean minimum average cost: so long as the marginal revenue remains above the marginal cost of production, there is money to be made by increasing production, even though average costs may rise. This is why governments apply excess profits taxes in wartime.

Later in the report, the Task Force suggests that "supply and demand means little unless the student sees how he can use them in understanding why farm surpluses persist in the face of government price support policies." Obviously, surpluses do not "persist in the face of government price support policies"; they are caused by government price support policies. (Otherwise low prices would drive enough farmers brankrupt to reduce production; just think, incidentally, what that would do to Common Market tariffs on American agricultural produce!) What is striking is the failure of acreage controls to reduce surpluses, and to understand this failure the student must know that the farmer, by more intensive cultivation of his land, can increase production per acre under conditions of developing agricultural technology. His marginal costs rise ("returns" diminish) in this process, but they remain below the support price, so he persists. Students who know only what the Task Force wants them to know will not be able to handle the question the Task Force asks them to handle.

EXAMPLE 5:
Page 47: "When the government spends more than it collects in taxes (creating a deficit), an increase in the public debt results."

Not true: governments, if they want to be really irresponsible, can just print money and spend it, as Brazil does, and as Nationalist China did in the year before its collapse. This deliberate inflation of the currency is a form of taxation: the currency in the hands of the populace is worth less because government expenditure has taken a bite out of each piece of paper. The notion of "forced saving" through inflation (ignored by the Task Force) is both interesting and important, and by no means irrelevant to what may happen when governments add to their debt figures by selling bonds to the central bank. It can easily occur, as the Brazilian and Chinese examples demonstrate, *pari passu* with rising unemployment.

EXAMPLE 6:
Page 53: "About two-thirds of the world's population has a very low per capita output—generally estimated at less than $150 per year."

This sentence presents with magnificent brevity the conventional abuse of Gross National Product analysis in cross-cultural situations. In American terms, a per-capita income of $3 a week (which is, of course, the highest the income can be on a per-capita output of $3 a week) leaves people without what to eat. Poor as the Task Force's two-thirds of the population undoubtedly is, most of it does have what to eat, and some kind of clothing, and roofs over heads—which is manifestly impossible on $3 a week.

What goes wrong is the market orientation of the measured Gross National Product, which deals essentially with money flows. Explaining GNP in a pamphlet, Lewis E. Wagner of the University of Illinois (who was chairman of the materials evaluation committee that worked at a distance from the Task Force) wrote that "If you pay a mechanic $15 to repair your car, production has taken place. . . ." He does not, however, mention that if you repair the car yourself the GNP never hears about it. (At a meeting of economists, Colin Clark once solemnly pointed out that GNP omitted the daily labors of housewives, though it included that of servants; a questioner with equal solemnity added that GNP omitted the *nightly* labor of housewives, though it included that of certain unattached females.) A high GNP is in part a function of the division of labor. Because people do different things for themselves in different cultures, per-capita GNP figures are not really comparable.

EXAMPLE 7:
Page 63: "Communist societies have not suffered from economic instability (booms and depressions) to the same extent that private enterprise economies have."

This sentence got the Task Force into no end of trouble, and deservedly so. The worst period of "depression" a modern nation has suffered came in "War Communism" in the Soviet Union; the 1930s in the United States pale by comparison to it. Soviet growth rates before World War II looked so good largely because the base line was taken at the bottom of this depression. In the late 1920s, the Soviet government abolished unemployment by law, thereby avoiding many of the apparent fluctuations that afflict capitalism. Gross misallocation of resources—which is the economist's view of unemployment—seems to have persisted, however. The Soviet error in the "virgin lands" policy is probably no less significant than the American error in overexpansion of steel and aluminum capacity at about the same time. The growth in Soviet GNP has not been steady, even accepting Russian prices at face value. An exploration of what the figures mean in terms of quality, durability, and originality of goods and services (GNP trouble, again) might indicate that Soviet "booms and depressions" from misallocation of resources are quite comparable to the capitalist experience. "The instability of profit-motivated investment which characterizes private enterprise economies" is not necessarily greater than the instability of decision making by a government planning group—even if this group is advised by the very best economists. One admires the Task Force for its courage in this section of the report but not for its definition of terms.

APPENDIX C

A Note on the Dedication

This book, which for this purpose should be a more distinguished piece of work, is dedicated to the memory of the late Francis Friedman, a particle physicist and professor of physics at MIT. He died in the summer of 1962, of cancer, at the age of forty-three. Though not many educators even knew his name, he was probably the one person American education could least afford to lose. A generation of children will be the poorer for his early death.

I did not know Friedman well. I saw him on perhaps five or six occasions, and only once, after his operation, sitting in a garden on a fine June morning, did we spend as much as an hour alone together. He was a tall man, cast in a classically American, lean, awkward mold, with a wedge of brown hair rising to the side over a long, lined, mobile face. He spoke softly, ironically, not at all eloquently, earnestly, always reaching for the piece of chalk to put on a blackboard. He knew about, valued and wrote clean, clear English prose.

He was a ferociously intelligent man, who did not care whether you knew it or not. He was extraordinarily gentle, patient but persistent, imaginative but intensely pragmatic, eager to be instructed or corrected by experiment and its analysis. In 1956, at the urging of his friend and colleague Jerrold Zacharias, he put these talents at the service of science education in American schools. He was the editor and in large part the author of the Physical Sciences Study Committee textbook; the most prolific single contributor of ideas for the startling PSSC films and laboratory devices; the most consistently perceptive analyst of the meaning of what happened when teachers presented first drafts of PSSC material to their students.

At the time of his death, Friedman was directing and inspiring an investigation of the extent to which younger children could work as scientists to learn science in the elementary grades. This project—aimed, incidentally, at developing a program for African as well as American schools—continues without him; but nobody pretends he can be replaced.

Before he turned so much of his attention to education, Friedman was regarded by his fellow physicists as a man of Nobel laureate quality, who would make a fundamental contribution to our understanding of the atomic nucleus. Future historians may find that he left behind him an even greater monument to his powers; our schools, our teachers, our intellectual community may yet justify the work and patience of Francis Friedman.

Index

Adolescents:
    fear of death, 153
    knowledge of self-ignorance, 130
    social studies, interest in, 165
Advanced Placement program 22-23, 46
    Amherst problems-in-history pamphlets, 45
    Modern European history, 42
Alexander, Sidney, 192
Altree, Wayne, 7
American Anthropological Association, 117
American Association of University Professors, 149
American Council of Learned Societies (ACLS), ix, x, xii, 73
American Economics Association, 93, 94, 99, 100
American Federation of Teachers, 14
American Historical Association, 23, 49
American History:
    Advanced Placement program, 24, students, 46
    classroom samples, 72-73, 126-128, 158-160
    geographical background, 31
    requirements, 42
    teachers, quality of, 21
    teaching, 42-43, "Posthole," 43-45
    texts, 7, 23, 31
American institutions—within framework of political theory, 185-188
American Political Science Association, 77
American public school, self-image, 155
Amherst pamphlets, 23
Anchor Science Study Series, 167
Anthropology:
    as behavioral science, 112-119

Anthropology—*continued*
    courses, 115
    Curriculum Study Project, 117-118
    goals, 112, 120
    greatest successes, 114
    -history, relationship, 113, 114
    jobs in, 165
    material of, 115
    natural science base, 110
    teaching, 118
    texts, 116-117, 176, "curriculum guides," 118-119
    universities and curriculum, 118
AP (*see* Advanced Placement program)
Archaeology:
    anthropology and, 115
    as approach to history, 56-58
    elementary school, 57-58
    Zilda P. Sibley Museum, 52-55
Association of American Geographers (AAG), 37, 38
Atamian, Alice, 12
Atlantic, 9
Auden, W. H., 40

Bach, G. Leland, 191
Baker, G. Derwood, 92
Bastert, Russell, 43
Beberman, Max, 18, 168
Behavior, man-animal:
    distinctions, 110
    similarities in learning, 172
Behavioral sciences:
    anthropology, 112-119
    method stresss, 111
    political science, 67
    psychology, 119-130
    sociology, 131-135
    terminology, 112

205

About the Author

Martin Prager Mayer was born in New York City in 1928. He was graduated in 1947 from Harvard, where he majored in economics and also studied philosophy and music.

After working as a reporter and editor for several publications he became, in 1954, a free-lance writer. He is the author of two novels and three reportorial studies, including *Madison Avenue, U.S.A.* and *The Schools.* Mr. Mayer's articles on business, law, music, audio, education, television and other subjects have appeared in *Harper's, The Reporter, Horizon, Esquire, Holiday, Life* and *Commentary,* among others.

In 1961-1962 Mr. Mayer served as a consultant to the American Council of Learned Societies and the Carnegie Corporation on the prospects for improvement in the teaching of social studies; *Where, When, and Why* is based on his report of his findings. Since November, 1961, he has been a member of the Panel on Educational Research and Development of the U.S. Office of Science and Technology. He is also consulting editor of *Programed Instruction,* the bulletin of the Center for Programed Instruction, as well as chairman of a New York City local school board and of the Board of Managers of the McBurney School.

Mr. Mayer is married to the writer and scholar Ellen Moers. They have two sons, Thomas and James.

Format by Katharine Sitterly
Set in Linotype Fairfield
Composed, printed and bound by The Haddon Craftsmen, Inc.
HARPER & ROW, PUBLISHERS, INCORPORATED